THE BIG BOOK OF OREGON GHOST STORIES

THE
BIG BOOK
OF
OREGON
GHOST STORIES

JANICE OBERDING

Globe
Pequot

Essex, Connecticut

Globe Pequot

An imprint of Globe Pequot, the trade division of
The Rowman & Littlefield Publishing Group, Inc.
4501 Forbes Blvd., Ste. 200
Lanham, MD 20706
www.rowman.com

Distributed by NATIONAL BOOK NETWORK

British Library Cataloguing in Publication Information available

Library of Congress Cataloging-in-Publication Data
Names: Oberding, Janice, author.
Title: The big book of Oregon ghost stories / Janice Oberding.
Description: Guilford, Connecticut : Globe Pequot, [2022] | Series: Big
    book of ghost stories | Includes bibliographical references. | Summary:
    "As the dense coastal fog rolls in to blanket the shoreline in gloomy
    silence, one thing becomes very clear. Oregon is a state in which ghosts
    roam. Not only here on the coast but in the lush green inland regions as
    well. Oregon is the ninth largest state in the United States and is one
    of contrasts. From the fertile Willamette Valley with its hundreds of
    wineries to its rugged coastline; from its twenty-two feet tall Pioneer
    statue, known affectionately as Gold Man, sitting atop the state capital
    in Salem to its ghost towns, Oregon is a state of stark beauty,
    hauntings, and history. Ghosts linger for any number of reasons. Those
    who've stayed in Oregon range from millionaires who refuse to move from
    their mansions, lonely cemetery inhabitants, and those attached to local
    theaters, saloons and hotels to ladies of the evening who made the wrong
    life and death decisions. Their reasons for staying put are as varied as
    there are rose bushes in the state"— Provided by publisher.
Identifiers: LCCN 2022005444 (print) | LCCN 2022005445 (ebook) | ISBN
    9781493066667 (paperback) | ISBN 9781493066674 (epub)
Subjects: LCSH: Ghosts—Oregon. | Haunted places—Oregon.
Classification: LCC BF1472.U6 O2348 2022 (print) | LCC BF1472.U6
(ebook)
    | DDC 133.1/29795—dc23/eng/20220218
LC record available at https://lccn.loc.gov/2022005444
LC ebook record available at https://lccn.loc.gov/2022005445

Special thanks to:
Tara Bohren

Rocky Smith
Director, Oregon Ghost Conference
Owner, Haunted Oregon City

Patty Evans
President, Monteith Historical Society

Crystal King
Communications Officer, City of St. Helens

Stephanie Hull
Event and Outreach Coordinator, Explore Lincoln City

Contents

Portland

Willamette Valley

Central Oregon

Northern Oregon

Southern Oregon

Eastern Oregon

Mt. Hood and Columbia River Gorge

Western Oregon

Oregon Coast

Foreword

Ghosts. The Afterlife. What comes next?! I have always had an interest in the notion of spirits and hauntings, and I suspect you have as well because you've picked up this book. Why do ghosts stay here instead of moving on? What is a ghost, and how can we understand one more fully? What happens to our energy once we leave our failing bodies behind? These are some of the questions we seek to answer as we strive to move the paranormal field forward.

Janice Oberding has been doing just that as a well-versed author of many books and a celebrated figure in the paranormal world of research and historical investigation. Janice has written more than 30 books about ghosts, true crime, and all things historical. In addition to her written works, Janice has been a guest on numerous television shows and documentaries and is a public speaker as well. I've had the privilege to know and to work with Janice for some 14 or so years as of this writing, and there is nobody who knows hauntings as thoroughly as she does.

Late in 2007, I entered the world of paranormal investigation and became the general manager for the *Ghost Adventures* Crew. In this role, I was fortunate to cross paths with Janice and cement a friendship that is rooted in respect. Over the years, I've researched and investigated countless haunted hospitals, asylums, prisons, brothels, ships, poor farms, museums, hotels, mines, cemeteries, bars, homes, and workplace buildings. I have had the opportunity to network with some of the field's most well-known television personalities and to see firsthand the often uncelebrated efforts of the paranormal investigators who work tirelessly to bring comfort and peace to folks all over the world who are needing answers. Janice is right at home with these celebrities, researchers, and investigators as a respected and beloved peer and mentor.

In this book of Oregon's haunts, Janice has pulled together a collection of stories that are captivating and fascinating. I was born and raised in Oregon, where I live to this day. I thought I had heard all the stories of places that will raise the hair on your arms, but I learned a great deal more in the reading of these chapters. From the self-proclaimed "Weird Portland" to the less populated corners of this great state, there are scattered tales of ghostly goings on and unexplained encounters. I have investigated many of the places you will find in this book, and I think you will find the pages practically turn themselves because the stories are so enthralling. And what a magnificent setting for ghostly encounters this state offers!

Oregon is rich in diversity and history, from its people to its outdoor wonders. You can find yourself in a beautiful evergreen forest surrounded by wildlife and waterfalls, and you can just as easily be in the high desert with lizards scurrying by and the sun beating down on your face. From the Columbia Gorge to the Oregon Caves, there are limitless adventures to be had. Start your day on the peaks of Mt. Hood and end it with your feet in the sand of the Oregon Coast. Wherever you roam in Oregon, it's possible you won't be alone. The many who came before us to explore and to stay may just make themselves known to you as your footsteps fall where theirs once did. A cool rush of air, goosebumps, or a flash of something out of the corner of your eye could all be those restless spirits sharing in your journey of discovery. And if you listen closely, you may just hear their whispers echoing through abandoned hallways or floating on the breeze.

Please read on and find yourself lost in the world of Oregon's mysterious places. But before you do, allow me to offer this important note from me the Oregonian to you the reader. The correct pronunciation of Oregon is ORE-uh-g'n (like organ with an uh sound in the middle) or ORY-gun if you prefer. It does *not*, however, end with "gone." This is a small but important distinction. I am imparting that bit of wisdom to you so that if you ever find yourself traveling our haunted highways, you'll be sure to say it correctly. And while you're here, be sure to leave that umbrella behind because you'll never see a true Oregonian with one. Rain runs off our backs like a duck or a beaver. And that, my friends, is a debate for an entirely different book on Oregon sports rivalries.

Tom McCall, former state governor, once said, "Oregon is an inspiration. Whether you come to it, or are born to it, you become entranced by our state's beauty, the opportunity she affords, and the independent spirit of her citizens." Perhaps you will find, as many of us have, that the "independent spirit" of an Oregonian does not just apply to the living.

Happy Hauntings!

Tara Bohren

Introduction

*A*s a dense coastal fog rolls in to blanket the shoreline in gloomy silence, one thing becomes quite clear: Oregon is a state in which ghosts roam. And they are everywhere. Ghosts are here on the coast, in the high desert region, and in the lush green inland regions as well. Oregon is the ninth-largest state in the US and is one of contrasts from the fertile Willamette Valley with its hundreds of wineries to its rugged coastline, from its 22-feet-tall pioneer statue, known affectionately as Gold Man, sitting atop the state capital in Salem to its ghost towns, Oregon is a state of stark beauty, hauntings, and history.

Oregon's history is rich and colorful. It's a history that includes many American Indian tribes like the Kalapuya tribes who've lived here thousands of years, the indigenous Chinook people (the Wasco, the Wishram, the Clackamas, and the Clatsop Nations) who were here on this land long before the 17th-century explorations by Spanish conquistadors. The early 19th-century arrival of Jedidiah Smith, followed by other fur trappers eager to sate the appetites of the European fur fashion, brought more non-natives to the region. The westward expansion would continue unabated. In 1804, President Thomas Jefferson sent Merriweather Lewis on a mission to explore land west of the Mississippi River. As his co-leader in the expedition, Lewis chose William Clark.

The trail forged by the Lewis and Clark expedition became known as the Oregon Trail. This trail would lead to the western migration of thousands of pioneers who settled in Oregon. Those who fell ill and died during the journey were hastily buried along the trail, their ghosts attesting to the hardships they faced.

As you will soon see, Oregonians enjoy theater. Throughout the state, from the world renowned Shakespeare Festival in Ashland to the Liberty Theater in Astoria, theater abounds—large and small. Naturally most of Oregon's theaters are home to a ghost or two. They are actors and actresses, unwilling to take that final curtain call, or starstruck theatergoers unwilling to abandon the magic of the theater.

Oregon is also a land of buried treasure. Fortune seekers from all over the world come to Oregon hoping to find treasure that's been lost. At least one such treasure is guarded over by a ghostly pirate. Then, as now, gold was a magical word. In 1851, three years after California's Gold Rush began, came news of the discovery of gold along the creek beds of southwest Oregon. This brought thousands of gold seekers to Oregon dreaming of wealth. Some found only death and despair. Unaware that time has passed they remain to this day, in or near, the crumbling ghost towns where they once lived.

In addition to its ghosts, Oregon has plenty to boast about; not every state can brag of having the Liberty Bell visit. Yes, the Liberty Bell. It happened in 1915 when the bell was being transported to San Francisco for display at the Panama-Pacific International Exposition. On July 15, 1915, the train stopped off in Salem and reportedly 40,000 people came to see the bell. Not every state can boast that one of its former residents has occupied the White House, but Oregon can. That presidential connection is Herbert Hoover the 31st president of the US. Hoover's parents died when he was a young boy, and he was sent to Newberg to live with his uncle John Minthorn in 1884.

Oregon is the 33rd state and was admitted to the union on Valentine's Day in 1859. Forty-nine years later on a gloomy Valentine's Day, a 215-foot schooner, the *Emily G. Reed* ran aground at Rockaway Beach. The captain had misjudged his distance from shore. Eight men died in the tragedy. The *Emily G. Reed* is but one of the many sailing vessels that wrecked off the jagged Oregon coastline. Many of those who perished in these accidents are said to still walk the coast.

Oregon's ghosts linger. These are their stories. They are fact and legend, borne of truth that morphed into tales passed down from one generation to the next. Are these stories all true? No one can truly say. The reason for this is twofold: Most ghost stories are anecdotal. Someone sees something out of the ordinary and tells someone else. In examining ghosts, particularly, as they relate to history, it is not always easy to separate fact from legend. Perhaps we shouldn't even try. First and foremost, ghost stories are meant to entertain.

Those who are too hasty in congratulating themselves for being able to separate fact from fiction or to call ghosts the figments of imagination are setting themselves up to be the first to experience the extraordinary. This is usually how it works with ghosts. Don't ask me why. I have no idea. In denial you may find yourself at what I like to call the point of discovery—a shadowy figure just on the edge of our peripheral vision or a cold chill that suddenly fills a room and announces a ghost. And if you listen carefully you may even hear a disembodied voice or an unearthly cry for help.

Apropos here are the words of editor Francis Pharcellus Church in his 1897 reply to little Virginia O'Hanlon whose friends questioned the existence of Santa Clause. They do not believe except they see. They think that nothing can be which is not comprehensible by their little minds. All minds, Virginia, whether they be men's or children's, are little.

Are ghosts real? I think so. And after reading this book you may think so as well. Oregon's ghosts come from all walks of life—and death. They range from millionaires who refuse to move from their mansions, lonely cemetery inhabitants, those victims of heinous crimes who seek justice in the afterlife, and those that attached to local theaters, saloons, and hotels to ladies of the evening who made the wrong life and death decisions.

Their reasons for staying put are as varied as their lives were. Perhaps they've chosen to linger because Oregon is special—an intriguing state. But don't take my word for it. Let's begin our exploration of the ghosts that reside in the boldly beautiful state of Oregon.

Portland

Portland is Oregon's largest and most populous city. It is, according to those who know about these things, also the state's most haunted city. Why not? In 2012 *USA Today* listed Portland as one of the 10 most haunted cities in the US.

Portland sits at the confluence of the Willamette and the Columbia rivers. In addition to its ghosts, the city has given rise to many rock bands, including Everclear and Paul Revere and the Raiders, and before you ask, yes Portland is named after Portland in Maine, which incidentally is Maine's most populous city.

So how did this city in the Pacific Northwest come to share the name of a city in Maine? Portland's two founders disagreed over what the new town should be called. Asa Lovejoy and Francis Pettygrove shared an equal land claim on this area known as the Clearing. As it was being platted into a new city, both Lovejoy and Pettygrove wanted the city named after their respective hometowns. Lovejoy wanted the new city to be called Boston, and Pettygrove opted for Portland. It was agreed that there would be a coin toss and the man with best two out of three wins would name the city. Pettygrove won. The penny that was used in the toss is known as the Portland Penny and can be seen at the Oregon Historical Society Museum.

As an avid reader I must tell you that Portland also boasts the largest independent bookstore in the world, Powell's City of Books. There are more than a million books here and a lot of them are about ghosts and hauntings. But so far there are no ghostly residents. Can you imagine a better place to haunt? I can't either.

Great cities have their nicknames. Portland is called Stumptown for the early 19th-century desecration of forests by migrants from the east; it is also known by another, perhaps more colorful nickname, the City of Roses, and it is the perfect place to begin our quest of the Beaver State's ghosts.

Danford Balch and the Ghosts of Forest Park

*S*ituated in the West Hills near downtown Portland, Forest Park is Portland's large 5,100-acre municipal park that offers much to outdoor enthusiasts, particularly hikers with its more than 80 miles of trails. Wildlife is abundant within its lush green serenity; many different species of animals and birds make their homes here in one of the largest urban forests in the US. It all sounds idyllic. And it is. But there is the other side of Forest Park. And that is the haunted side. This is the darkness where ghosts are said to wander in the quiet hours just before daylight overtakes the city.

To facilitate the westward migration of settlers to the Oregon Territory, the US Congress enacted the Donation Land Claim Act of 1850 (also known as the Donation Land Act). Taking advantage of the act, Danford and Mary Jane Balch came west and settled onto their 345 acres with their nine children. Today Forest Park is where the Balch homestead once stood.

It's doubtful that Danford Balch set out to make Oregon history when he arrived here with his family. And surely, given the choice he wouldn't have wanted to be any part of the history he made. But Balch did make history. His 1859 execution marked the first legal hanging of the Oregon Territory. None of this might have happened if Balch hadn't hired the son of a neighbor to help him around his property.

From there it's an age-old story of love at first sight; young man working for the father falls in love with the daughter. In this case it was 18-year-old Anna Balch and 23-year-old Mortimer Stump, and they were besotted with each other from the moment they met.

As romantic daydreams filled their lives, marriage quickly became their goal. Doing the right thing as demanded by that era, young Stump went to his employer and asked for the fair Anna's hand in marriage. To Stump's amazement, the request enraged Danford Balch. For whatever reasons, Balch was vehement in his refusal to even consider such a thing. Stump was beneath the fair Anna and unfit for her in Danford's eyes, and he wasted no time in telling young Stump just this. When he'd finished his tirade, Balch ordered Stump to leave the farm at once and never to return.

But love is sometimes blind, heedless, and reckless. Determined to have one another, Anna and Mortimer snuck off one night and were married. And this set the tragedy in motion. While Mary Jane shrugged her shoulders at her daughter's marriage, Balch was brokenhearted. How could his dutiful daughter disobey him so? The more he pondered the situation, the angrier he became. If not for Mortimer Stump none of this would have happened; he was the cause of all the trouble; and he must pay for his treachery.

On November 18, 1858, Balch and Mary Jane went to Portland. Still seething at the way Mortimer Stump had stolen his daughter, Danford carried a double-barrel shotgun with him in case he encountered Stump. While Mary Jane shopped, Balch spent his time drinking at the nearest saloon. The encounter Balch hoped for happened that afternoon as his daughter and her new groom were boarding the Stark Street Ferry to cross the Willamette River.

Stump helped Anna to her seat then turned to see his father-in-law raise his shotgun. Stump never heard the blast that took his life. The *Daily Alta California* newspaper from November 29, 1858, reported Balch's murder of Mortimer Stump.

> A heavy charge of buckshot taking effect in his neck, almost literally shooting his head from his body.

Balch managed to escape but only for a short time. Six months later, he was captured and taken to jail. Rumors, as they always do in such cases, flew. According to one tale, Balch and his daughter Anna had long been involved in an incestuous relationship, and it was jealousy that drove his hatred and murder of Mortimer Stump. Legend has it that Danford Balch claimed his wife Mary Jane was a witch and that she had bewitched him into killing the son-in-law. The jury didn't believe a word of it. And after a short trial, it didn't take them long to find him guilty of murder and sentence him to death. Balch was hanged on October 18, 1859, eleven months to the day of the senseless killing of Mortimer Stump. This was Oregon's first legal and public execution.

It was reported that Anna Stump, the daughter Balch had cruelly made a widow of, was among those who witnessed his execution. True or not, this wasn't the last of Danford Balch, the ill-fated Mortimer Stump, or his young widow Anna. According to local lore, the unlikely trio continues to haunt the area where the Balch family home once stood. For many years now, ghost enthusiasts have been visiting an area near Balch Creek at Forest Park in hopes of encountering the ghostly Danford, Anna, or Mortimer.

Known as the Witches Castle for Mary Jane Balch, who some believe practiced witchcraft, the stone structure is the remnant of public bathrooms built here in the 1950s. Those who have encountered the ghosts of Danford Balch say he is miserable and unhappy with the way his life on Earth ended. But so is the ghostly Mortimer Stump, who doesn't appear as often as Danford. Mary Jane remarried after her husband's execution and lived here on this land with her new husband for the rest of her life. She seems content with her ghostly residence.

Anna is the saddest of the four ghosts connected to the Balch case. The young widow never recovered from the murder of her husband. Her restless ghost sobs and shrieks as she makes her way through this wooded area of Forest Park ever in search of her beloved Mortimer.

Ghost researchers believe that strong emotion and a sudden unexpected or violent death may give rise to a haunting. This being the case, there may be other ghosts here besides Anna Balch Stump. Reports of disembodied sobbing and screams echoing through Forest Park, are numerous.

This may be because murder has come here several times since Danford Balch built his family home. In 1960, two college students were savagely murdered in the park while parked in an area known as a lovers' lane. The murders went unsolved for several years. In 1996, a woman was slain on one of the trails by her ex-boyfriend who was later convicted of the crime. In 1999, the bodies of three women were discovered in separate secluded areas. Todd Alan Reed, known as the Forest Park Killer, confessed to the murders and was convicted and sentenced to three consecutive life terms.

Ghosts at Lewis and Clark College

*A*ccording to legend, the ghostly action at Lewis and Clark College takes place during the early hours of the morning in an outdoor area in the center of the campus. On certain nights, when conditions are just right, a lone ghost will tear through the grounds letting a bloodcurdling scream fly. In hot pursuit is a large group of ghosts. Who are they and why are they chasing this ghostly man? If you should ask any of them, they will all vanish as quickly as they appeared. But don't take it personally.

They will be back tomorrow night or the following night or the next after that. This sighting is most likely a place memory or a residual haunting that is a traumatic event that's been imprinted on the surroundings. For most, there is no interaction, just as there is no interaction between a television show and a viewer. However, there are some who claim to have been roughly shoved by ghostly hands while waiting for the ghosts to appear. This might fall under the Be-Careful-What-You-Ask-For heading.

Shanghai Tunnels

If you've ever watched David Giuntoli as Nick Burkhardt (the Grimm) battling supernatural creatures throughout the Portland area you've heard the notorious Shanghai Tunnels mentioned more than a few times. If you're a ghost hunter, the Shanghai Tunnels is probably on your bucket list.

Said to be extremely haunted, the tunnels were originally built by Chinese laborers so that goods could easily be transported from Portland's docks to the basement of local businesses. Laden with goods, ships sailed from the Pacific Ocean into the Columbia River and onto its tributary the Willamette River and docked in Portland. After a ship was unloaded, it wasn't unusual for a captain to find himself with a dwindling crew. This is when he might turn to extreme measures. In his 1849 semi-autobiographical novel Redburn, written two years before his classic Moby Dick, Herman Melville said of those who shanghaied:

> Besides, of all seaports in the world, Liverpool, perhaps, most abounds in all the variety of land-sharks, land-rats, and other vermin, which make the hapless mariner their prey. In the shape of landlords, barkeepers, clothiers, crimps,* and boarding-house loungers, the landsharks devour him, limb by limb; while the land-rats and mice constantly nibble at his purse.

Although some historians argue that although this did occur in other parts of the world, it seldom happened in Portland and certainly wasn't a regular practice. Still, legend has it that when a large enough crew couldn't be secured legally, men were drugged and shanghaied (kidnapped) in the bars and taverns of Portland.

---

* Crimp was another word for someone who shanghaied.

These unlucky men were then taken through underground tunnels to awaiting ships where they would be sold as crewmen, who were forced to work—or else. Joseph "Bunko" Kelly was well known for shanghaiing unsuspecting men. According to legend, Kelly shanghaied more than 2,000 men and occasionally women as well. He found 20 of his shanghai victims near death in a mortuary they'd broken into. The men had mistakenly helped themselves to embalming fluid thinking it was liquor. Kelly loaded them all the same into carts and took them to the ship's captain, explaining they were drunk and drugged. He was paid for his services and the ship sailed down the Columbia River with its corpse crew. And Kelly resumed shanghaiing men through the tunnels.

Death was a common occurrence there in the tunnels. A man who attempted to fight back against his captors might be murdered, and his body left to wither and rot where it fell. Occasionally a victim might break free and try to escape, but he wouldn't get far. Eventually he would be overcome and disoriented in the darkness, and he'd lose his way only to perish in the tunnels.

The ghosts of these unfortunate people are said to wander the tunnels to this day, the sounds of their hysterical sobs echoing through the long-forgotten areas of the tunnels. The ghosts of shanghaied men who went to watery graves in ships that sank in the Columbia River also roam the tunnels. A person, who had the chilling experience of encountering one of these ghosts during a tour, described him as being taller than average with glowing red eyes and a stench that was so powerful it took his breath away. That's a ghost you may not want to run into.

But he's not the worst to inhabit the tunnels. There are ghosts lingering in the tunnels who like to push and shove anyone they don't happen to like.

In 2012, the *Ghost Adventures* (i.e., Zak Bagans, Nick Groff, and Aaron Goodwin) visited the Shanghai Tunnels to film an episode of the TV show. What they encountered during filming may lend credence to the stories of unsuspecting men being drugged and shanghaied.

Brentwood's Ghostly Fiasco

*I*n spring 1922, Mr. and Mrs. Herbert Wellcome moved into a small house in the Brentwood section of Portland. It wasn't long before they found themselves being harassed by the machinations of a ghost. Neither of them was getting much sleep. Ghostly rappings, slamming doors, and other unearthly noises were keeping them up at night. Was it a ghost—or something else? In desperation, the Wellcomes sought the help of Deputy Sheriff Christopherson who came to investigate. After an hour at the residence, he could find neither a ghost nor anything amiss.

When word got out about the bothersome specter, neighbors offered their advice. Perhaps it was a dog under the house wagging its tail or maybe a woodpecker. There was no dog and there was no woodpecker. And the noises continued. The next time he visited the house, Deputy Sheriff Christopherson, like a good ghost hunter might, brought assistance. Christopherson and the three deputies entered the house ready to find the ghost—perhaps others had missed something they might discover. After a thorough investigation the four men reached a sexist conclusion, Mrs. Wellcome was creating the noises herself.

Mrs. Wellcome denied their accusations and turned elsewhere for help. Dr. D. Chambers, an optometrist and member of the American Society for Psychical Research, went to the Wellcome home to discover what was causing the manifestations. Dr. Chambers concluded that the phenomena was that of a poltergeist;* further, he believed the Wellcomes were the victims of a persecution similar to that suffered by so-called witches in Salem, Massachusetts. Dr. Chambers further went on to state:

---

* *Poltergeist* is a German word meaning noisy ghost.

As to the strange happenings that have taken place at their little home in Brentwood let me state in the first place that neither Mr. nor Mrs. Wellcome knew anything about ghosts. Nor were either of them Spiritualists and this experience was an entirely new experience for them. . . . I will add that the phenomena under discussion are designated by psychical research societies as poltergeist.

The Wellcomes were vindicated and eventually packed up and moved out of the Brentwood house. There was no word on what became of the poltergeist.

Piggott's Folly

It is natural to be good; unnatural to be bad.
—Charles Henry Piggott

A 1920 article in the *Oregon Daily Journal* newspaper referred to Piggott's former home as a haunted castle. Calling it Mount Gleall because that is what Piggott himself called his castle in a combination of his children's names (Gladys, Earl, and Lloyd), the article stated that Piggott claimed Queen Victoria and an assortment of other ghosts had appeared in an earlier photo of the surrounding area of his castle.

Charles Henry Piggott left San Francisco and came to Portland in 1877. He worked at several jobs before becoming a lawyer and a writer. Fifteen years after coming to Portland, Piggott established the Union Brick Company. When planning to build his new home, he decided on an unusual castle design. There were no right angles in the interior of the castle and legend has it that this prevents evil spirits from gathering. The eccentric Piggott may have been aware of this. In his 1908 book, *Pearls at Random Strung; Or Life's Tragedy from Wedding to Tomb: Including the Scientific Causes of All Diseases, Poverty, Premature Death and Longevity,* Piggott discusses many topics including ghosts and the afterlife, as he saw it.

The Piggott family would happily live in the four-bedroom, three-bath house for a year before it was lost to foreclosure in 1893. In 1909, several years after the Piggott family moved out, New York artist, Théodore Gégoux abandoned his wife and family in New York and mysteriously vanished. A year later, he was in Portland and living in Piggott's castle. Since that time several people have lived at the castle. Today it is a private residence, and this means do not disturb those who live here.

Is the castle as haunted as rumor says it is? Does the ghost of Charles Henry Piggott still keep a lonely vigil in his castle during the early morning hours?

Rose at the White Eagle

For of all sad words of tongue or pen, the saddest
are these "it might have been."
—John Greenleaf Whittier

The White Eagle Saloon and hotel is more than a hundred years old; this makes it one of Oregon's oldest bars. It is also one of Portland's most haunted locations. Situated in one of Portland's oldest sections, near the Shanghai Tunnels, the White Eagle is one of those bars where unsuspecting men were drugged, taken through the tunnel, and forced to work on departing ships.

Popular with Portlanders from the beginning, the White Eagle was built in 1905 and opened as a saloon by Polish immigrants, William Hryszko and Barney Soboleski. They named their bar after the stylized white eagle that appears on the Polish flag. According to some stories Hryszko and Soboleski expanded their business by operating a brothel and illegal gaming upstairs and an opium den in the basement at the White Eagle. Rose is believed to be one of the women who plied her trade at the brothel. Nothing ever went Rose's way; she was one of those people that misfortune seems to follow.

And then she fell in love with a married sailor. Suddenly it looked as if her luck had finally changed. The sailor loved her madly and vowed to leave his wife for her. He might have done just that, and they might have lived happily ever after. It might have been, if only the ill-fated Rose hadn't been murdered by a drunken customer.

Still hoping for the return of her sailor, Rose continues to haunt the White Eagle to this day—and night. A sudden drop in ambient temperature and the fragrance of sweet floral perfume subtly announce her presence. When not feeling so subtle, the ghostly Rose can be heard sobbing loudly upstairs.

Aside from Rose, the victims of shanghaiing occasionally come back to the White Eagle. The rowdiest ghosts are those who died while being forced through the tunnel. Watch your step. One of these ghosts has been known to reach out and grab people as they climb the stairs.

Keep a close eye on the bartender. He may well be the ghost of a long-dead employee who doesn't want to leave his bartending duties behind. And much to the dismay of the other bartenders, he is known to move bottles and glasses around.

Ghost Ship on the Willamette River

> The Moon was a ghostly galleon tossed upon cloudy
> seas.
>
> —Alfred Noyes

*T*here's something mysterious and ghostly happening here on the
Willamette River late in the night. If you listen carefully you may
hear the mournful sound of a foghorn. This is your only warning.
And it is heard just before the ghostly ship makes a brief appearance
only to vanish into the thick murky fog.

Some believe the spectral ship is the steamer *Gazelle*. Five years
before statehood was granted to Oregon, the two-engine side-
wheeler *Gazelle* was put into service in spring 1854. A month later,
on April 8, 1854, the steamer sailed into Oregon history in a disastrous way.

Shortly before seven in the morning, the *Gazelle* neared Canemah
on the east bank just above the Willamette Falls. The steamer
crossed the river and pulled alongside the steamer *Wallamet* docked
nearby. There the *Wallamet*'s crew swiftly loaded freight from their
steamer onto the *Gazelle* and it moved away.

The *Gazelle* was a little more than a hundred yards from the
Wallamet when a thunderous roar tore through the steamer as it
was ripped apart by a catastrophic boiler explosion. The explosion
instantly killed 20 people, including the pilot of the *Wallamet* who
was killed by a piece of shrapnel; 27 others suffered horrific injuries
and four of them would later die of their injuries.

In what would be the Pacific Northwest region's worst such
disaster, witnesses told of rescuing the injured and of the river
bloody strewn with body parts and pieces of the steamboat. Those
who survived suffered broken bones and severe burns.

Perhaps the steamboat *Gazelle* is the ghostly ship that makes a brief appearance on foggy nights. And those who perished in the horrific explosion all those years ago may still be haunting this area of the Willamette River. If so, perhaps it isn't a foghorn at all but only the pitiful moans of men whose lives were tragically cut short through no fault of their own.

Lone Fir Pioneer Cemetery

Here we lie by consent after 57 years, 2 months and
2 days sojourning through life awaiting nature's
immature laws to return us back to the elements of
the universe of which we were composed.
    —Tombstone of James and Elizabeth Stephens,
        founders of the Lone Fir Pioneer Cemetery

*N*ot every cemetery is haunted. But the Lone Fir Pioneer Cemetery certainly is. Established in 1854, it is the oldest cemetery in
Portland. Approximately 20,000 people are buried in this peaceful
green space just across the river from downtown Portland. The lone
fir tree, for which the cemetery was named by Aurelia Barrell, is still
standing tall among several other species of trees. Lending beauty
and an aura of tranquility are some of the oldest roses in the state of
Oregon and that is fitting in the City of Roses.

The idyllic surroundings change when nightfall comes because
that's when the ghosts come out. Unearthly moaning and screaming is heard throughout the cemetery and an ethereal woman in
white has been seen flitting among the tombstones. Speak kindly
and reach out to her; she will turn and flee. She may be the ghostly
Charity Lamb who lies in an unmarked grave here. She made history for being the first woman convicted of murder in the Oregon
Territory.

In 1852, Charity, her husband, and their four children left North
Carolina and headed west. The arduous journey along the Oregon Trail took them five months. But once settled in Oregon, they
received a land patent for 318 acres.

On Saturday evening, May 13, 1854, Charity decided she'd finally
had enough. She was tired of her husband Nathanial Lamb's cruel
and endless torment. There was little recourse for abused wives in

the 19th century, and Charity suffered horrendous abuse from her husband who thought nothing of hitting and kicking her. This was a time when women were supposed to suffer silently—not Charity; she realized that she must put a stop to her husband's mistreatment of her.

So she made a decision to take matters into her own hands. Subtlety was not her strong suit. She waited until the family was seated around the dinner table, and then she calmly picked up an axe and struck her husband twice—the blows were sufficient to kill him.

When lawmen caught up with her at a neighbor's house, Charity said, "I didn't intend to kill the critter, only to stun him."

Regardless of her intent, Mr. Lamb was dead. Newspapers reported the murder as inhuman, revolting, and cold-blooded.

On the day of her trial, the *Oregon Spectator* newspaper reported that Charity Lamb was emaciated as a skeleton, with an abstracted, sad, and downcast look.

There were no women on juries in 1854 Oregon. If there had been, Charity might have received a less severe punishment. Two of the Lamb children testified that their father often beat their mother. The twelve-man jury was not swayed. They found Charity guilty of second-degree murder and then urged the judge to show her mercy. She was sent to the Oregon State Hospital for the Insane. She died there in 1879 and was buried in an unmarked grave.

In 1930 Charity Lamb's grave and those of Chinese immigrants and patients who had died at the state hospital were covered over with cement. In 1952, believing that all the bodies had been removed, the Multnomah County erected a county office building on the spot there in the southwest corner of the cemetery.

But they were wrong. The bodies were still there, buried beneath the building. The county only discovered their mistake 50 years later in 2004 as they were preparing to sell the land to real estate developers. Once this was proven, the county building was demolished and work began on a memorial for the Chinese laborers and the patients at the state hospital who rested here alone and forgotten in an area of the Lone Fir Pioneer Cemetery known as Block 14.

If you're the sort who seeks out cemeteries on rainy nights and you should come here to the Lone Fir Pioneer Cemetery, be prepared. You just might encounter the ghostly Emma Merlotin (Anne Jeanne Tingry-LeCoz), a beautiful French prostitute who was murdered on such a night in 1885. There is nothing shy about the ghostly Emma who is elegantly attired in the French fashion of a century ago. The distraught ghost will appear near her grave screaming loudly. If you look closely, you will notice that one of her eyes is missing. An explanation for Merlotin's missing eye was offered on December 31, 1885, in the *Coast Mail*:

> There is a popular delusion, based somewhat on scientific facts, that an image of the last object upon which a person dying suddenly looked, remains upon the retina after death. In the vain hope that examination, under the photographer's lens of the retina of the murdered woman's eye would reveal a likeness of her slayer, one of the eyes was cut out yesterday and placed in the hands of a well-known photographer. It is expected that a negative proof will be obtained today.

On December 22, 1885, three days before Christmas, a killer visited Emma at her little cottage. He had come to rob and murder her. She didn't realize this until it was too late. She fought valiantly for her life, but the killer wielded his axe so skillfully, so brutally, that she didn't stand a chance. Alerted by her pitiful screams, the police arrived moments after the killer fled. The cottage was covered in blood. Emma was beyond earthly help. A reward of $700 was offered, but the killer was never caught and the murder went unsolved. And this may be the reason Emma Merlotin cries out on cold rainy nights.

Archie Brown (Eugene L. Avery) and James Johnson are also thought to be among those who roam these grounds on moonless nights. Brown and Johnson shot and killed Louis Joseph, a young boy, while fleeing a constable after committing a robbery. Both men were convicted of murder and sentenced to death. On March 15, 1879, Brown and Johnson were hanged on the same scaffold. The togetherness doesn't end here. The two men were also buried in the same unmarked grave.

Nearly half of those that are buried here at Lone Fir rest in unmarked graves. Others were moved here from a nearby cemetery several years ago. Ghost experts will tell you that this can be upsetting and could well be the reason for the shadowy ghostly sightings that occur here.

Before we call it a night at the cemetery, let's look at one of the most famous residents here. This would be the unfortunate, Asa Lovejoy, who lost that coin toss for the honor of naming his new city. There is no record of Asa's ghost hanging around; yet I wonder who the ghostly gent in frock coat and top hat might be.

The Ghostly Woman of Multnomah Falls

> Passed several places where the rocks projected
> into the river & have the appearance of having
> separated from the mountains and fallen into the
> river, small niches are formed in the banks below
> those projecting rocks which is common in this
> part of the river, Saw 4 Cascades caused by Small
> Streams falling from the mountains on the Lard.
> —Merriweather Lewis, October 30, 1805

*M*ore than two million people visit Oregon's Multnomah Falls each year. There are good reasons for this. The falls is picturesque, and with a height of 620 feet, it is the tallest in the state. And it's only 30 minutes outside of Portland.

The Missoula floods that occurred at the end of the last Ice Age more than 15,000 years ago were the largest on Earth in the last two million years. With a flow that was 10 times the combined flow of all the Earth's rivers, the raging flood of melting glaciers swept surging water across Idaho, eastern Washington, and Oregon and down the Columbia River Gorge. This catastrophic event formed Multnomah Falls.

While this is the likeliest explanation for the creation of the falls, American Indian legend offers another story of how the falls came to be. And it is from this legend that our next story springs.

Helplessly watching as her people died one after another from the mysterious illness that was threatening to wipe out her tribe, a beautiful young Multnomah maiden realized she must do something—but what? The elders had told her that the Great Spirit was so angry with her people that he had sent the plague as punishment. She loved her people and would not stand by and see any more deaths.

There was only one way to save them all from certain death: A sacrifice must be made. And after two days of agonizing thought, she knew what she must do. As the chief's daughter, she must be that sacrifice. It was the only way.

Her mother and father begged her to reconsider; let someone else's daughter be the sacrifice, they pleaded. She was resolute. She'd seen enough suffering and death. And no one, not even the young man she loved, could change her mind. She waited until nightfall and then climbed to the top of the highest cliff and dove headlong to her death. When they discovered her battered body the next morning, her people wept for her sacrifice, asking the Great Spirit for a sign that she had not died in vain.

Within days that sign came: People had recovered and were well again. This is when the falls began to form. But there is more to this story.

By sacrificing herself, the young woman ensured herself a place here at the falls forever. According to legend, she returns during the winter. Those who've seen her say that she solemnly gazes into the distance. Known as the ghostly woman of Multnomah Falls, she wears a glowing white dress and appears just below the historic Benson footbridge. Look into the water; her face has been seen in the waterfall or just beneath the water's surface.

Some say they can feel her presence, and her overwhelming sadness, as they walk across the bridge.

Buttermilk Bluebeard and the Ghosts of Heathman Hotel

The eyes only see what the mind is prepared to comprehend.

—Henri Bergson

*T*he Heathman Hotel was built in 1927. Eighty-three years later the hotel was featured in the racy film, *Fifty Shades of Grey*; there is no telling what the ghosts thought of that.

The elegant old hotel offers 150 luxurious rooms and suites and doormen dressed as beefeaters. But let's not forget the aforementioned ghosts. Those that haunt the Heathman are said to have an affinity for rooms and suites whose room numbers end in three. No explanation as to why this is has been offered. We do know that the ghosts here are mischievous and attention seeking. To that end they have been known to rearrange furniture in certain suites and to destroy otherwise clean rooms when the occupants are out for the day or evening.

The ghost of a woman who committed suicide by jumping from a top floor is believed to be in residence. Apparently, she regrets her hasty decision. In the wee hours of the morning, her pitiful sobs can be heard in certain areas of the hotel. The sobs could also be those of Marjorie Stoy who died here at the hotel under mysterious circumstances in 1928.

Stoy was a young woman who had recently separated from her husband of 10 years. Free from the responsibilities of marriage and a husband, she began dating other men. She and George Masterson met at a local nightclub, and two hours later she accompanied him back to his room at the hotel. Masterson's promise of a good time and an illicit drinking party seemed just the sort of fun Marjorie was looking for. So there she and Masterson were in room 330 at the

Heathman Hotel—drinking, dancing, and having a good time. Prohibition was in full swing and bootleg booze parties were all the rage with those who just wanted to have some carefree fun.

At this point in her life, a good time was all Stoy wanted. Unfortunately, her partying didn't end well. The morning after the party, a maid found Marjorie's naked body sprawled across the bed in Masterson's room. When they finally caught up with him three days later, Masterson claimed the death was an accident. Regardless he was arrested for Stoy's murder.

A bullet to the heart had ended all of Marjorie's fun. Or had it? Marjorie may be the sobbing ghost. But she doesn't stay sad for long. She is believed to be the smiling ghost that's been seen in different rooms throughout the hotel. Without a care in the afterworld, she continues happily cavorting through the hotel.

There is yet another ghostly resident, and she is not as cheerful as Marjorie is, and she has good reason for this. She is Isabelle Van Natta, who was cruelly murdered in her room by a cold-blooded killer in 1945.

A nasty chill hung in the air as a cold gray November day became an even colder night. It was two days past Thanksgiving, Saturday, November 24, 1945; Alfred Cline stepped up to the desk of the Heathman Hotel and registered as Mr. and Mrs. Alfred Cline. His wife stood waiting a few feet away. It was already dark, and she was tired.

Mrs. Cline was smartly dressed for a woman of a certain age. But she was obviously several years older than her husband and walked with the assistance of a cane; this was unimportant to her husband. She had a nice fat bank account and that was all that mattered. Forget what the poets said of feminine wiles; it was her money that first attracted Alfred to Delora, and numbers in a bank account were everything to Alfred.

After a quick courtship, Alfred and Delora were married, and suddenly Cline was living a life of luxury. The elderly Delora was madly in love with her charming much younger husband. She truly was blessed. He was such an attentive and wonderful man. After all, they'd met at church where he sang in the choir. Delora may have been head over heels in love, but her relatives weren't so easily convinced.

A honeymoon was in order and Alfred convinced his bride that they should visit Oregon. So the newlyweds traveled to Portland where Alfred prepared to put his scheme into action. But there was a snag, something Alfred hadn't expected. When his wife was recognized by an old friend, Cline knew he must act fast. Five days after he and his bride checked into the Heathman Hotel, he carried out his nefarious plan.

Cline never deviated from his routine. Why should he when it had always worked out perfectly. He and his bride would take a little honeymoon trip and check into a luxurious hotel. Once his wife had signed everything she owned over to him, Cline offered her a glass of buttermilk, telling her what a refreshing drink it was. Invariably she drank—and invariably she died. Cline would then locate a doctor who would sign the death certificate, no questions asked. The body would be shipped out of state and cremated, thus destroying the evidence of the poison spiked buttermilk.

Upon Delora Cline's death, all her earthly possessions went to Alfred. Now her relatives demanded answers from Delora's new husband, and as it turned out, the woman who was murdered at the Heathman hadn't been Delora because Cline had murdered her shortly after the wedding. But with Delora dead and forgotten in Texas, he needed a stand-in to take her place in Oregon until he could complete his forging of all her documents. This is where the unfortunate Isabelle Van Natta came in.

Cline's was a convoluted scheme of seeking lonely and very wealthy widows, wooing and marrying them. Soon after the wedding he would then have them sign all that they owned over to him. Blinded by love, and eager to please their new husband, women happily signed. This of course was their death warrant because once he had their signatures on the dotted line, he wasted no time in murdering his brides.

When the truth of Cline's crimes came to light, he was dubbed the Buttermilk Bluebeard. Authorities believed he was responsible for the deaths of at least 11 people. And yet, he was never convicted of a single murder. There simply was not enough evidence. Cline was too cunning for that. With his victim's bodies cremated as quickly as possible, there was no way to prove how they had died.

But not to worry, justice is a different sort of lady—one that Cline couldn't escape. He was convicted of nine counts of forgery. The judge ruled his sentences should run consecutively; thus, he was sentenced to 126 years at California's Folsom Prison. He died there of a heart attack in 1948.

Looking at the cruel way they exited this world, is it any wonder that the ghosts of Heathman Hotel are sometimes mischievous?

Nina at Old Town Pizza and Brewing

And, though I was a soul in pain,
My pain I could not feel.

—Oscar Wilde

Located above the Shanghai Tunnels in the historic Merchant Hotel building in Old Town is the Old Town Pizza and Brewing, which offers great pizza and beer—and the ghostly Nina. Nina, it is said, was a young prostitute working in the building circa 1890s.

Her story is a familiar one. Nina was weary of the life she was leading. She was making plans to leave her life as a prostitute and make a new start. In doing so, she angered the wrong person. And for that she paid with her life. Her broken body was found at the bottom of the elevator shaft where she'd been thrown. Although there were suspicions as to his identity, the killer was never apprehended. Nina was buried and forgotten—only she wasn't.

Nina refused to leave the building where she was murdered. Ghosts don't have the same concept of time that the living do. Unaware of the passage of time, Nina is still hoping to come face-to-face with her killer. They say her favorite spot is in the basement. Nonetheless, she makes herself comfortable throughout the building. Like so many other ghosts Nina makes people aware of her presence with the strong fragrance of sweet perfume.

Just to be certain she's not overlooked, Nina has also appeared on the stairs. Her chosen attire is black and she rarely smiles. If someone still doesn't realize there's a ghost in the house, Nina's been known to touch the individual she thinks isn't giving her the attention she deserves. That ought to startle someone into realizing that Nina is nearby.

Some may say that Nina's story is more legend than fact. No doubt they will see things differently once they've encountered her.

The next time you stop in at Old Town Pizza and Brewery for an awesome beer and 'za, make sure you pronounce Nina's name correctly while speaking about her. Her name is pronounced Nigh-na and not Neena. Nothing irritates the ghostly Nina more than to hear people mispronouncing her name. And who wants to try and eat a slice of pepperoni goodness with an irritated ghost hovering over their table?

Rimsky-Korsakoffee House

Portlanders understand and appreciate how
differently beautiful is this part of the world.

—John Reed, 1914

*F*or all its other charms, Portland is a city of eclectic coffee houses.
One of these is the Rimsky-Korsakoffee House.

As you may have already guessed, the coffee house located in an
old Victorian house at 707 SE 12th Avenue is named after Russian
composer Nikolai Rimsky-Korsakov. Locals call it Rimsky's, and yes,
they serve some luscious homemade desserts and coffee. Won't you
be seated? Every table is named for a long-dead classical composer,
and in the evenings, live classical music is performed.

The place or at least some of the tables are said to be haunted.
There's some general weirdness going on with glasses falling from
the tables for no reason and a table that seems to vibrate. It's possible that the ghosts are Louise Bryant and John Reed.

If you've seen the 1981 movie *Reds*, you know about the life of
socialist journalist John Reed and his wife, writer, and activist Louise
Bryant. Legend has it that for a short time during the early 20th century, the pair lived here in this house. According to biographer Mary
V. Dearborn in her book, *Queen of Bohemia: The Life of Louise Bryant*, they were introduced to each other here at the home of Eva and
Norma Graves. Either way, they didn't stay long. Because of their
socialist political views, Bryant and Reed traveled to Russia where
they covered the 1917 October Revolution for the curious back in
the US. Reed wrote *Ten Days That Shook the World*, and Bryant
wrote from a woman's viewpoint for magazines and newspapers.

Reed died of typhus five days before his 33rd birthday on October
17, 1920. The Portland native bears the distinction of being the only

foreigner buried at the Soviet Union's National Cemetery, Kremlin Wall Necropolis, in Red Square.

After Reed's death, Louise traveled the world and eventually remarried. Neither she nor her new husband was happy in the marriage. Even after the birth of their daughter, they couldn't agree on anything—especially Louise's drinking. There was no way the marriage would last. After their divorce, Louise continued her downward spiral into alcoholism.

She was 51 years old when she died on January 6, 1936. She is buried at the Cimetière des Gonards in Versailles. In death, 2,000 miles separate Louise and John. But time and distance are nothing to ghosts. Although neither John Reed nor Louise Bryant claimed to favor Portland, the romantic among us might imagine the two lovers returning in ghostly form to the place where their romance began.

And here at Rimsky-Korsakoffee House at a table tucked away in the corner, they smile at one another as they once did, sipping coffee and enjoying classical music. . . . And perhaps they do.

The Screaming Bridge

*F*or decades now, her ghostly cries have risen up from Cathedral Park beneath St. John's Bridge and echoed through the night. She is Thelma Taylor, Portland's most famous ghost.

On August 5, 1949, Thelma, who was 15 years old, was waiting for the bus to Hillsboro where she hoped to get a summer job, a job that would buy her all the things that teenage girls covet. Morris Leland put a stop to all Thelma's plans when he forced her to accompany him to a secluded spot beneath the St. John's Bridge.

There he held her captive overnight. The next morning Thelma heard men working in the nearby trainyard and started calling for help. Leland panicked. He was an ex-convict with no intentions of going back to prison. To silence her screams, he beat her to death with a steel bar and then stabbed her lifeless body several times before burying her in a shallow grave.

Five days later, Leland was arrested in a stolen car and readily confessed to the grisly murder. The entire state was outraged at his heartless crime. Thelma Taylor had been a popular and well-liked student at Roosevelt High, and she warranted justice. During his trial, Leland pled not guilty by reason of insanity; the jury didn't believe a word of it.

Leland's case was appealed all the way to the US Supreme Court. He did not prevail. On November 19, 1952, Morris Leland appeared in court to hear the date of his execution.

"I'm just as well off dead as being in any penitentiary or jail in this state," Leland sullenly told the judge.

"Conditions at the penitentiary are uncalled for. The food is no good and there is no decent heat," he added.

Leland shouldn't have worried about the heat. No doubt he was destined for a much hotter climate when on January 9, 1953, he was executed in the gas chamber at the Oregon State Penitentiary at Salem.

Thelma, they say, haunts Cathedral Park to this day. The ghostly young woman is never seen. But on warm summer nights, her bloodcurdling cries for help can clearly be heard throughout the park and on the bridge; so clearly in fact, that police have been summoned to aid the screaming woman.

Of course, they never find a victim. Those who've been on the job awhile have come out to the park before. They know that they will not find the screaming woman; she is a ghost and beyond any earthly help they might offer.

Brenda and the Ghosts

*M*y friend Brenda H. is just one more reason I like Portland. We met at the Washoe Club in Virginia City during an event to celebrate ghost-hunting friends, Mark and Debby Constantino, who had died tragically in a murder-suicide the year before. Naturally when ghost investigators get together, the talk is ghosts and hauntings. When writing a book about ghost stories it's a given that a writer will ask their friends about experiences with ghosts. Knowing that Brenda has had some interesting encounters with the paranormal I asked if she might share some of them. The following are a few of her ghostly experiences.

In 2008, I found myself single with two young daughters. I went back to school, and as you can imagine, life was crazy busy. One afternoon during this time, I went to visit a friend who lived about 40 minutes away. It was dark and rainy when I got ready to drive home. I have horrible vision at night, and it would be impossible to drive without my glasses, so I know I was wearing them during the drive home.

The next morning, I was getting ready for school and couldn't find my glasses. I always put them on my nightstand next to my bed, but they weren't there. I had them when I got home because there is zero way I could have driven home without them. I tore my house and my car apart looking for them; I even went through the garbage. I was so stressed with everything going on that I chalked it up to me losing them. This was early fall. There was nothing I could do but get new glasses, and this really pissed me off at myself.

That same year my daughters were at their dads' for Christmas. Being newly single and alone for the holidays I didn't even bother to decorate. The following Christmas I pulled the horrible pull ladder down in the garage, navigated over old ski equipment, boxes that my dumbass ex didn't take with him. It took me 30 minutes to find the five holiday boxes and another 30 to get them down the ladder. As I was going through the boxes and deciding what I was willing to put out and what I was going to put away, I came across a box that had old decorations and stuff from my childhood, things I hadn't used for many years. There in the middle were my glasses with not a bit of dust on them and the typical fingerprint on the right lens that I always had to clean off.

Around 2010, I start dating a detective for the Portland Police Department. He was sane and rational. It was a new relationship, and I hadn't yet introduced him to my children. The first time he stayed the night with me at my house, my daughters were with their dad. I set my alarm for 5 a.m. because he was working dayshift. When the alarm went off, I noticed he wasn't next to me in bed. I went looking for him and found him asleep on the couch in the family room. I nudged him awake and offered to make coffee.

In the kitchen, he hugged me and kissed my forehead.

"I really like you Brenda, but there's no way I'm ever staying in this house again," he said.

Shocked, I asked, "Why do you say that?"

"Every time I fell asleep last night, a man's voice would say, 'You don't belong here, you need to leave.'"

I chuckled and asked, "Did it sound like this?" And laughing, I repeated his words in a deep demon voice.

He didn't laugh. "I'm serious," he said. "The man's voice was pleasant, but the message was clear."

We dated for a while longer, but he never did come back over. He was always creeped out about my house.

In 2013, I was visiting a girlfriend in Henderson, Nevada. We were planning on going out that night, and I took a shirt out of my suitcase to show her what I planned to wear. I put it back and we spent the day lounging by her pool. When it was time to get ready that night, I opened my suitcase and the shirt wasn't there. I couldn't find it. My girlfriend is OCD about organization; she went through my suitcase and looked under the bed and even in the laundry room. It was nowhere to be found.

A few days later we were driving to Oregon and stopped in Virginia City for a Bloody Mary at the Bucket of Blood Saloon. The new phone I'd bought in Las Vegas was charging in the car. I unhooked the phone from the charger, leaving the new white charging cord in the USB outlet. We had two Bloody Marys, walked around a bit, and went back to the car. I took my phone out to put it on the charger and the cord wasn't there. I looked under the car, in my purse, and in the restroom at the Bucket of Blood. But it was gone. I went to Reno and bought a black off-brand charging cord.

I am organized and wasn't happy with myself for losing the new white cord. The rest of the drive to Oregon I was not in the best of moods. Two days later, we arrived in Portland and pulled up to my house. We both needed to use the restroom, so we ran into the house. As we walked past my laundry room I stopped and looked at the laundry basket. There on top was the shirt I'd shown my girlfriend in Vegas and the white cord I'd lost in Virginia City.

In 2015, I was cleaning house and noticed a pair of old children's wire-framed glasses on my nightstand. I asked my daughters where they came from, and they said they had never seen them before. I ignored them for a few days, but the longer I thought about it the more this bothered me. I have a friend that is a medium. I met with her just to have lunch, and as an afterthought, I pulled the glasses out of my purse and put them in front of her and asked her what she thought of these.

I assumed that she would tell me some story about a young girl that owned them that was now a old woman. She picked them up, and it was like they burned her because she dropped them so fast onto the table and said, "Oh god, these just showed up, didn't they?" I said, "Yes." She said, "No, I mean one second, they weren't there and the next they were, correct?" I said, "Yes." She just stared at me for a second and she then started explaining that everything in our universe is the same age. The fruit you eat, the car you drive, the furniture from IKEA, and every cell in your body was created at the exact same time; they have the same vibration. She held up the glasses and said this is new to this universe, it just got here. Spirits or loved ones are in a different plain or universe. Someone is trying to get me to open my eyes regarding something. It must be important because this doesn't happen often.

She told me that when you open your eyes to whatever they are trying to tell you, don't be surprised if these cute little things go missing. I still have them (weird, that my glasses disappeared a few years prior).

In 2018, I decided to sell this huge house. My oldest daughter moved in for a while and helped me get it packed and ready to sell. The living area was on the main level, and downstairs was a huge family room and a couple bedrooms. It drove me nuts being downstairs hearing someone run down the hallway. Sounded like the ceiling would cave in. I had a crazy mom rule about NO F---ING RUNNING!! It was 10 p.m. the first day of packing stuff up, and my daughters were downstairs watching a movie. We heard what sounded like some-one running and stomping from the master bedroom to the kitchen and back down the bedroom. It was louder than I had ever heard. I thought it was my oldest daughter that had went out that evening coming back home. I was pissed at the crazy stomping!!

My two daughters said, "Holy shit, Jaclyn's in trouble."

I called her cell and asked, "What the hell are you doing?"

"I am having a beer at Puffs; come on down, momma," she said.

"You didn't come home just now?"

"Nope."

My daughters knew something wasn't right; they were staring at me. I thought maybe my son had come in. Not wanting to scare my daughters, I said, "It's your brother."

I walked upstairs, and the doors were locked and windows secure. No one was up there. As we progressed with packing, I started notic-ing we were blowing lightbulbs daily.

This is a six-bedroom home and lightbulbs were only lasting three hours. By the time we moved out, I was not buying more light bulbs, and there was one that was left in the downstairs bathroom. I knew at that time we had something more than an electrical prob-lem. Oddly I wasn't scared at all, just diligent on whatever it was wasn't going to scare my daughters. If they had freaked out, I think then I would have. Three days after moving out, my neighbor called me and said, "Hey do you have the lights on a timer?" I said, "No." "Well, every light is on in the house and the blinds are open."

I went back over and went in by myself and felt like an idiot but said, "Listen, I lived here for 15 years and have had some great memories, please stop with the lights. You may scare the new owners and they will be getting the keys in a few days. Be nice and move on, please!"

I am close with the neighbors across the street and the family that moved in has a foster home for children, and they love the house and have had no issues. Thank God! I personally feel that whatever was there was not wanting me to move and tried to protect me. I call the energy a "him" because it was a man's voice that my boyfriend heard. He obviously didn't think this man was right for me. I believe he's been with me for a long time. My ex-husband suffered from horrible night terrors—until we divorced.

Ha ha ha, I'm not even sad about that.

Brenda's story of the disappearing and reappearing glasses, shirt, and cord may seem odd to some, but it is a common enough occurrence in the paranormal. Frustrating as it sometimes is, ghosts are notorious for moving items around. I have lost small items only to find them in exactly the spot I had previously looked for them. This phenomenon is called *apport phenomena*, when an item suddenly appears in a different location from where it originally was.

Many years ago, a friend, who is a medium, told me of having a steak tag with the word medium apport in her shoe. And during a stay at the infamous Myrtles in Louisiana, my late friends Mark and Debby Constantino and I were called to another guest's room. There we were told that an apport had resulted in a bejeweled western belt appearing in the room. The belt looked like an ordinary belt of that type, the person involved seemed sincere, and there was no reason to doubt his story.

If apport phenomena have your interest peaked, you might want to check out the Scole Experiment.

Benson Hotel

We make a living by what we get, but we make a life by what we give.

—Winston Churchill

Simon Benson was a self-made man. He and his family emigrated from Norway to the US in 1868. Young Simon Berger Iverson changed his last name to Benson and quickly set about building a business and making money. In 1879, at age 28, he moved to Oregon and started buying forest land along the Columbia River. Eventually he would own more than 46,000 acres.

By the time he reached the age 60, Benson was a wealthy man indeed. A philanthropist who generously donated to the city, Benson was a teetotaler and gave Portland $10,000 so that 20 bronze drinking fountains could be installed. Thus, he hoped to keep people away from alcohol during their lunch breaks. Known as Benson Bubblers, more than 50 of these unique four-bowl fountains are still in use in downtown Portland. Step up if you're thirsty.

Benson had always kept himself active. When he retired, it wasn't to sit in his rocking chair and reminisce about the past. He still had a dream. And that was to build an elegant first-class hotel in the heart of Portland. He hired well known Portland architect Albert E. Doyle to design the hotel. On March 5, 1913, Benson saw his dream come to fruition with the opening of the Oregon Hotel. More than a million dollars had been spent building and furnishing the hotel. Benson hadn't reckoned on failure. For all its grandeur, the hotel was not being managed well and lost money during the first year. Unwilling to see his dream die altogether, Benson forgot retirement, stepped in, and took over the hotel's operation and changed its name to the Benson Hotel. Under his management the hotel succeeded. Still living the dream, Benson sold the hotel six years later.

The Benson Hotel is still elegant and still going strong today, albeit with a ghost or two in residence. In fact, in 2014 *USA Today* proclaimed the Benson Hotel to be one of the most haunted hotels in the world.

The November 12, 2008, death of John Graham "Mitch" Mitchell, former drummer with Jimi Hendrix, is ironic in that it is believed that Mitchell died of alcohol-related problems in the hotel built by a teetotaler. Mitchell was in town to perform in the 2008 Experience Hendrix Tour when he died in his sleep in his room at the Benson.

Some believe Mitchell has extended his stay at the hotel indefinitely. He might not be playing his drums, but he is playing plenty of pranks. Don't be surprised if your things get rearranged while you're sleeping. If you're one of those people that is hoping to experience a ghost, keep in mind that most of the ghostly activity happens on the 7th, 9th, and 12th floors. Apparitions have also been spotted on the grand staircase. One of them is none other than Simon Benson himself. The ghostly Benson always appears in elegant evening attire. He smiles and acknowledges those who've noticed him. And then he casually strolls down the stairs—still living the dream in the afterlife.

The ghostly Benson gets around and wanders throughout his hotel. Occasionally he will angrily topple a cocktail or a bottle of wine. Those who've seen him say that he looks as real as you or me. Other ghosts roaming the hallways at all hours of the day and night include a ghostly little boy and a woman in white. Those who've come across the ghosts of the Benson Hotel say they are the friendly sort, and there is nothing to be afraid of.

I'll drink to that, but not when the ghostly Simon Benson is around.

Murder at the Starry Night

There is no torrent like greed.

—Buddha

*R*oseland Theater in Portland is haunted. Some believe he is the ghost of a man who was murdered there more than 30 years ago. In one of Portland's greatest mysteries the question is—where's the body?

By the late 1980s, Larry Hurwitz was on top of the rock music world. He'd converted an old evangelical church in a rundown section of town into the city's largest and most successful nightclub that he called Starry Night. The venue was drawing crowds. And big names were appearing there, including Bob Dylan, Ray Charles, Metallica, Boy George, John Lee Hooker, and Tina Turner.

There was only one problem. The city fire marshal had set a strict limit on the number of people that could occupy the nightclub. This clashed with Hurwitz's greed; he wanted as many people in Starry Night as he could cram in. Because tickets were numbered and counted, he started making counterfeit tickets so that he could bring more people into the nightclub. It was a lucrative scheme until that night in January 1990.

During John Lee Hooker's performance on January 20, promoter Tim Moreau discovered Hurwitz's scheme. He confronted Hurwitz who tried to convince him to keep his mouth shut. But no amount of talk could dissuade Moreau from going to the authorities. There was no way out. Hurwitz decided that Moreau must die. Three days later, he killed Moreau with the help of a friend and drove the body to a secluded area on the Washington side of the Columbia River Gorge and buried it.

Ten years later, friends turned on Hurwitz. When they got done telling what they knew, Hurwitz pled no contest to the murder charge. He was convicted and sentenced to 12 years for the murder of Moreau, even though the body has never been located.

Today the Starry Night is known as the Roseland Theater. And the ghost of Tim Moreau roams the premises; he's said to give those who encounter him a cold chill. He's been spotted numerous times since that night in 1990. You may wonder why he is here since his murder was solved, and he received a certain amount of justice.

Perhaps he just enjoys the music, or he wants someone to come and finally discover his body in its lonely grave up in the Columbia River Gorge.

Pied Cow and Buttertoes

One cannot think well, love well, sleep well if one
has not dined well.

—Virginia Woolf

I've always thought that Buttertoes is an unusual name for a
restaurant. But then again, Buttertoes was an unusual restaurant.
Located in the historic J. C. Havely House at 3244 SE Belmont, the
unique eatery was operated by three sisters who filled it with fairy
tale décor and toys. The walls were adorned with fantasy murals of
mermaids and fairies. An early mermaid painting by noted Portland
artist, David Delamare, also graced a wall. Keeping with the theme,
every item on the weird and whimsical Buttertoes menu was named
after a fairy tale.

The Portland mainstay was also haunted by the ghost of an
elderly woman known as Aunt Lydia. There was nothing mean or
threatening about the ghostly aunt. Still some employees claimed to
be creeped out while in her presence, especially when she decided
to knock things off kitchen shelves and move things around.

With the possible exception of ghosts, nothing lasts forever. Buttertoes with all its delicious recipes is long gone. The restaurant
ceased operations in 1983. But not to worry, the Pied Cow coffee-
house and hookah lounge took up residence in the J. C. Havely House
and apparently the ghostly Aunt Lydia is perfectly content with the
new establishment. Maybe she is thrilled with the menu at the Pied
Cow, which includes coffees, teas, pies, cakes, and a banana split.

Although some deny the existence of Aunt Lydia, others insist
they've heard her walking up or down the stairs—and yes, she
still wants things her way. When something isn't where she thinks
it ought to be, she wastes no time in rearranging it. What did you
expect from a persnickety ghost?

Riverview Cemetery

Destiny is that which we are drawn towards and Fate is that which we run into.

—Wyatt Earp

*A*lthough he only visited Portland once during his life, Virgil Earp, brother of the legendary frontier marshal Wyatt Earp is buried here in Riverview Cemetery. His daughter Nellie Jane was living in Portland when Virgil died of pneumonia in Goldfield, Nevada, in 1905. Nellie Jane couldn't bear to have her father buried in a dusty western town so far away, so she sent her son-in-law to Goldfield to bring Earp's body to Portland for burial. Although Virgil doesn't make appearances at Riverview, he's said to haunt the Arizona town of Tombstone nearly every night. So as the ghostly Earp wanders the streets of Tombstone in search of the OK Corral, other ghosts roam Riverview.

Twelve years before Earp was buried in Riverview, William S. Ladd was buried there. Ladd, who was elected as Portland's fifth and youngest mayor, went on to become a successful businessman and to create the cemetery he now rests in. Little did any of his mourners suspect on that cold January day in 1893 that Ladd would rest peacefully, but four years later, his body would be pulled from its casket and held for ransom.

> The body of William S. Ladd, the Portland millionaire who died in this city in January 1893 has been taken from its resting place in Riverview cemetery, and is now in the hands of ghouls, who are doubtless holding it for the sole purpose of securing a reward for its restoration.
>
> *The Dalles Times-Mountaineer*, May 22, 1897

43

The body-snatching scheme didn't work out as planned. The men involved were arrested, convicted, and sentenced to long prison terms. The body was returned to Riverview. To prevent any further ghoulish ideas, the Ladd family built a concrete mausoleum to hold the patriarch's body.

Paul Bunyan and the Kenton Ghost

Paul Bunyan is the hero of lumber camp whoppers
that have been handed down for generations.
These stories, never heard outside the haunts
of the lumberjack until recent years, are now
being collected by learned educators and literary
authorities who declare that Paul Bunyan is "the
only American myth."

—W. B. Laughead

*P*aul Bunyan, the larger-than-life lumberjack and his companion
Babe the Blue Ox are folk heroes throughout the US and Canada.
If there was a giant tree that needed to be felled or an entire forest,
the legendary Bunyan was your man. Or so the story goes in the
timberlands.

Bunyan was such a popular man that the town of Kenton wanted
to honor him. For the 1959 commemoration of Oregon's Centen-
nial, Kenton commissioned a 31-foot-tall Bunyan statue to be built.
Kenton began as a company town for Swift Meat Packing Company,
so surely the town would get some long overdue notice with the finished statue.

In 1913, decades before the giant Paul Bunyan was erected, Kenton was being talked about for a different reason. There was a ghost
in Kenton. And its descriptions varied significantly. Depending on
who was telling the story, the ghost was either that of a rather skinny
man or a hefty man. So many prominent people claimed to have
seen the phantom that ghost hunts were organized in hopes of cap-
turing it or at least getting rid of it. The newspaper reported that the
ghost was usually spotted near Patton Road and Lombard Street. As
more people came forward with their own ghost encounters, William Adams told a reporter that he had spotted the ghost sitting on

a tree stump. He approached the ghost in a friendly manner and attempted to carry on a conversation with it.

Instead of replying to Adams, the ghost turned and vanished. Try as they might no one could get the ghost to acknowledge them, much less talk with them. Whatever his reasons for being in Kenton, the ghost kept to himself. The Paul Bunyan statue was placed on the *National Register of Historic Places* in 2009. There is no word on what became of the Kenton ghost.

Pittock Mansion

It's as much fun to scare as it is to be scared.

—Vincent Price

California has its Winchester Mystery House and Oregon has the Pittock Mansion. Although some of the ghosts in residence at the Winchester Mystery House are not especially friendly, those at Pittock Mansion are congenial. You see, Henry and Georgiana Pittock are still happily in residence here in their mansion after more than a hundred years. Perhaps happiness in the hereafter is the key to being a friendly ghost.

Their 46-room mansion was a showpiece when completed in 1914. And the Pittocks eagerly moved into their new home in the West Hills with breathtaking views of downtown Portland. Here they would live with their two married daughters and their families. Although the Pittocks were elderly, they kept busy with their many interests. Avid gardener, Georgiana was the founder of the Portland Rose Society and a founding member of the Portland Rose Festival.

Henry and Georgiana also shared a passion for women's rights. They worked for women's suffrage in Oregon and advocated for women's right to vote. Sadly, when the 19th Amendment giving women the right to vote was finally passed in 1920, Henry and Georgiana Pittock were long dead. But they weren't necessarily gone or forgotten.

The city of Portland purchased the estate for $225,000 in 1964 and opened it to the public as the Pittock Mansion Museum a year later. This is when it was discovered that the Pittocks hadn't gone far. Visitors and staff insist that they are still here in their mansion. In life, such a large estate needs a staff, so it is the same in the afterlife. The apparitions of a gardener and a housemaid have also been encountered at the Pittock Mansion.

Many people have seen, or heard, ghosts in different locations of the mansion. The most active are Mr. and Mrs. Pittock who smile in acknowledgment when they are spotted. The aroma of old-fashioned rose perfume, just what you'd expect from the woman who loved roses, can be noticed when Georgiana is about. Footsteps and windows and doors that open and close on their own are some of the ghostly activities that take place at Pittock Mansion. Oh, and I should tell you that Henry and Georgiana have also been spotted throughout the mansion they loved; home sweet home, indeed.

The Crystal Ballroom

Where there is no heart there is no art.

—Anna Pavlova

*D*ance instructor entrepreneur Montrose Ringler's Cotillion Hall was built in 1914. Ringler, who is credited with having brought the tango to Oregon, liked dancing and believed that it was good for one's health. His new dance hall was lavishly decorated and fitted with a ball bearing and rocker floor called a "floating floor." The floor was said to bring a new sensation to Portland dance.

Whether or not that was true, Cotillion Hall caught the eye of policewoman Lola Baldwin, superintendent of the Portland Police Bureau's Women's Protective Division. Baldwin, who was one of the first policewomen in the US, was not impressed. She considered saloons and dance halls as places where young women's reputations and lives could easily be ruined. In her zeal, Baldwin fought to have Portland close down dance halls, including the Cotillion Hall.

Ringler fought against her efforts. In 1921 he welcomed jazz, which was quickly becoming popular. This new type music, he thought, could change the world of dance. Still, not everyone agreed with this. That same year, Ringler was arrested for operating the Cotillion Hall on a Sunday and for not having a license. He gave up his lease on Cotillion Hall, and he and his family moved to California; Baldwin retired in 1922 as well.

New owners came and went. One of them changed the name to the Crystal Ballroom, and the building slowly fell into disrepair. It would be many years before it was restored to its original glory. This started in 1979 when the city decided the building was worth saving. The McMenamin family stepped in and created a brewery, a bar, a restaurant, and a floating dance floor for the Crystal Ballroom, making it a Portland showpiece—a haunted showplace if you will.

A lot of emotions and energy passed through this building. It's no wonder that some of those who visit the Crystal Ballroom encounter the paranormal. The apparition of a young woman in a sparkling white gown is what people usually report seeing. Perhaps she is a ghostly debutante hoping for a do-over of her coming out party. Others hear the sounds of ghostly laughter, footsteps, and whispering. A few have been tapped on the shoulder by an icy unseen hand. Possibly this is a ghostly young man that escorted a debutante to her first dance. And he is only asking, "May I have this dance?" Hmm. This makes me wonder what it would be like to take the white-gloved hand of a tux-wearing ghost and to dance with him on a floating dance floor.

KWJJ Country Music and a Ghost

Where there is no imagination there is no horror.
—Arthur Conan Doyle

*T*his is Portland. And clearly, Portland has it all—even a haunted radio station. Radio station KWJJ moved into the Wilcox Mansion in King's Hill district on Halloween 1957.

It wasn't long before those who worked for the station were reporting apparitions, a swinging chandelier, and strange noises. In his book, *A Ghosthunter's Guide to Haunted Landmarks, Parks, Churches and Other Public Places,* author Arthur Myers told of interviewing employees and former employees of KWJJ. The ghostly figure of a female servant was seen throughout the mansion as she went about her work. Dressed in clothing from the 1920s, she seemed oblivious to anything but the task at hand.

It was the shadowy figure of Theodore Burney Wilcox, the mansion's original owner, that was most often spotted in the mansion. Standing near the staircase as if he was observing what was happening in *his* home, Wilcox appeared to almost glow in his white top hat and tuxedo. He occasionally sat on the bench and played the piano. Maybe Mr. Wilcox didn't care much for the station's music play list and was making his feelings known.

His thoughts on the musical matter may have been shared. In the 1970s, the station changed its format from easy listening to country music. And that has worked out well. Today KWJJ is known as 99.5 the Wolf. The station is no longer housed at the Wilcox Mansion, and there is no word as to whether any of the ghostly residents of the mansion moved along with KWJJ.

New owners and offices have since moved into the mansion. Only time will tell if Theodore Burney Wilcox chose to remain somewhere in his large and lovely haunted abode—and maybe, just maybe a few of his ghostly pals stayed on as well.

Beware of Movie Stars Selling Neckties

*F*rankly my dear, local lore has it that before he slipped into his Rhett Butler frock coat and cravat, Clark Gable sold neckties in the men's wear department at the Meier and Frank Department store in downtown Portland. The year was 1922, and he was 21 years old, working here only until he could fulfill his dreams of becoming a famous actor. It didn't take Gable long to make the move from Meier and Frank to Hollywood. But some believe that he's returned and is happily still there—demonstrating neckties.

When asked about this at a recent paranormal event I had to admit that I couldn't see the ghostly Gable doing this, not after he reached the zenith of stardom. Besides, he is said to haunt Hollywood hotspots of yore with a number of glamorous women. But nothing is impossible in the realm of ghosts. So it well might be that Gable is one of the ghosts who haunt the Meier and Frank building. Hopefully he is looking for a well-fitting coat and not selling ties. Gable liked Oregon. There are two other places he enjoyed getting away to once he became famous. The Weasku Inn on the Rogue River at Grants Pass and the Wolf Creek Inn were favorite relaxing spots of his and wife Carole Lombard's. So, I'm betting if Gable is haunting anyplace in Oregon it's one of these aforementioned inns.

But there are other ghosts at the Meier and Frank building. A translucent woman that walked back and forth through women's wear was seen many times before the store finally closed its doors forever. The ghostly woman folded and unfolded neatly stacked clothing. That seems like monotonous work. We can only hope she finally realized that her shift was over and called it quits.

There is yet another dedicated employee who is said to stay on at the former department store. The ghostly janitor is occasionally seen as a shadowy man who goes about vacuuming, whistling, and watching the clock—will this shift ever end? Someone needs to tell him to punch his timecard and be done with it.

Willamette Valley

The 150-mile long Willamette Valley extends from Portland in the north to Eugene in the south. The Native Kalapuya people are believed to have lived in the Willamette Valley for more than 10,000 years. Today 70 percent of Oregon's population lives here. It's safe to say then that many of Oregon's ghostly residents also reside here in the Willamette Valley.

Ghost in the Deb Fennell Auditorium

*W*hen I first heard the name Deb Fennell, I assumed the auditorium was named after a woman—a woman named Deborah, a no-nonsense person who, wanting to get right down to the job at hand, called herself Deb. I could almost see her, nails nicely manicured, hair elegantly coiffed, and the de rigueur stylish phone case. Then I started to do some research. And that's when I discovered that my psychic abilities were in need of some fine tuning. Delbert Fennell was a local Tigard football player who went by the name Deb; so there it is, the logical reason the haunted auditorium at Tigard High School is named after the local star athlete who went on to become a highly respected educator and the Tigard school superintendent.

Schools are rife with ghost stories. Students and staff are always in the know about such ghostly goings on. If you should ask them at Tigard High, they will tell you there's a ghost at the Deb Fennell Auditorium. He is believed to be a former student who worked in the auditorium. As with most ghost stories, there are a number of tales relating to his death. One story has the teenager heartbroken over losing his girlfriend. No matter how he tried to win her back, the young lady preferred the company of another boy. Deeply depressed, he crawled up to the catwalk and hanged himself. Another story has him dying in a horrific head-on car crash on a rain slick highway. And yet another tale has him accidentally falling to his death from the catwalk.

Regardless of how he met his demise, the ghostly young man stays on in the auditorium. His footsteps can be heard at all hours of the day and night. He has been known to hide things and to play with the light switches. Some claim to have seen his tall shadowy apparition standing in different locations throughout the auditorium. They say that if they call out to him, the lights will flicker as in response.

They Didn't Believe in Ghosts

*T*he July 20, 1912, issue of the *Oregonian* carried an interesting article titled "Ghostly Figure Gone; Estacada Officers Mystified by Adventure." The two men, A. G. Ames, city marshal, and Hugh Jones, deputy, made it clear that neither of them believed in ghosts. Disbelief has never stopped someone from encountering a ghost, however. Besides, there was a good chance that Ames and Jones may have seen one.

Late one evening, the two officers were patrolling the park in Estacada on the bank of the Clackamas River. It was a quiet night, overhead the clear and cloudless night sky was filled with stars. As they always did, the men carried on a friendly conversation while they walked. When they came to a path that led down to the water, they stopped and suddenly fell silent. The water was as smooth as glass, starlight reflecting on it.

Something in the distance had caught their attention. A man, wrapped in a blanket limped toward the water's edge. Suddenly he dropped the blanket and jumped into the water with a loud splash and was gone. Was he drunk or sick? Ames and Jones ran toward the spot.

The water was still, and there was no sign of the man in the water or on the riverbank. Then one of them said to the other, "Do you remember Beers, that saloon fella that drowned himself last week?"

The other man gasped, "Why this is that exact spot!"

"Yes, and did you happen to notice that the one we just saw walked like Beers."

Had they seen the ghost of the man who'd committed suicide at this spot? Or was it only a coincidence? Neither of them would ever speak of the incident again. But after that night, neither Ames nor Jones could ever be certain that ghosts didn't exist.

The Little Girl on Croisan Creek Road

It's Friday night. And if you happen to be out driving in Salem, I'll offer words of warning: Don't speed, especially on Croisan Creek Road, unless you want to encounter a ghost. Legend has it that a little girl was killed by a speeding hit-and-run driver long ago on a lonely stretch of this road. Unaware that she is no longer of this Earth, the ghostly child haunts the road to this day. Those that drive faster than the posted speed limit have reported seeing a ball roll out into the road, followed by the little girl.

Once the car is stopped, the ghost retrieves her ball and dissolves in a haze. Some of those who've witnessed the ghostly little girl have also seen a little boy who stares forlornly from the side of the road. They could be the specters of two children who were killed on Croisan Creek Road or just a couple of ghosts who've wandered onto the roadway. Either way, they've been here a long time and have become part of local ghost lore.

Argyle Winery

Not dead, but gone forever.

—Headstone of Lena Elsie Imus

Zachariah and Hannah Imus ran the Dundee Post Office. When her father died in 1907, Lena Elsie Imus felt duty-bound as the Imus's only unmarried daughter to leave school in Portland and return to Dundee to help her mother in the post office. In Dundee, Lena met and fell in love with a man who would change her life.

On December 19, 1908, while other young women looked forward to Christmas, 25-year-old Lena made a tragic decision. She took a bottle of carbolic acid down from a kitchen shelf and crept upstairs to her bedroom. There, she sat down on her bed and drank the poisonous liquid. It was the pitiful ending of an age-old story; when Lena discovered she was pregnant she happily shared the news with her lover, but rather than marry her, he cruelly ran away, leaving her alone and scared.

Few things were worse than being an unwed mother in puritanical 1908. And Lena couldn't face the shame. Her mother was devastated at her daughter's death. She'd lost her husband the year before and two of her eight children in 1902. She buried Lena near her father in the Dundee Cemetery and life moved on.

In 1987, nearly 80 years after Lena took her own life, vintner Rollin Soles founded the Argyle Winery here. And wouldn't you know it? The winery implemented the house Lena once lived in as the tasting room. It didn't take long for the ghostly Lena to spring into action. She announced herself with the sweet aroma of perfume and moved wine glasses (empty and full) before the startled eyes of those enjoying a sip of Chardonnay. Perhaps after all her years of roaming this place, the ghostly Lena was delighted to have people around her once more. She is a mischievous ghost and has been known to frighten those who aren't expecting to encounter her.

Some ghost researchers might recommend banishing a prank-playing ghost. Alas that task is not as easy as you might think. It's a moot point here; the Argyle Winery has no intention of trying to chase Lena away. Those who know about such things say it's just as well not to go to all the trouble.

The winery has increased its varieties of wine and, in Lena's honor, named her old house the Spirithouse. A new tasting room has been built on the property. The winery throws an annual Halloween party as a way to acknowledge the ghostly Lena who continues to haunt the winery.

Oenophiles or not, doesn't a winery seem like a much more fun place to spend eternity than a cemetery?

South Eugene High School

It is your ordinary everyday high school; there are thousands of similar schools across the country, with one exception: There's a ghost here at South Eugene High School and his tragic story has been told for decades. The school was built in early 1950, and according to local lore, the ghost of Robert Granke haunts the auditorium.

On March 11, 1958, Granke, a 16-year-old theater department student, was replacing a light in the catwalk above the theater auditorium. Not a difficult job if one was careful. Granke had done it before. But on this day, he allowed his mind to wonder, lost his footing, and fell 55 feet. Students in the auditorium that morning stared in horror as Granke crashed into the theater seats, breaking his neck on impact, and dying instantly.

For the curious, the seats where Granke died were number 10 and 11 in Row G. Don't say I didn't warn you; those who've sat in these two seats have reported feeling a sense of foreboding. Apparently the ghostly Granke wants his presence acknowledged. He's been known to speak to students and call them by name, turn lights on and off, and move things around. Some have heard piano music coming from the locked auditorium and when he's nearby the room temperature drops noticeably.

An article by Kristin Sheley in the October 28, 1997, issue of *Oregon Daily Emerald* states that in an accident eerily similar to that of Granke, a workman fell through the catwalk during a 1994 remodeling of the auditorium. The workman survived, and this, many say, is because Granke's ghost saved him from the same fate he met on a long-ago spring morning in 1958.

University of Oregon, Eugene

Basketball arena McArthur Court saw its first basketball game on January 14, 1927. A lot of games and cheering and stomping took place in the home of the Ducks before it was replaced by Mathew Knight Arena in 2011.

All that energy may be one reason it is said to be one of the haunted locations on the University of Oregon campus. According to local lore, there is something ghostly lurking at Mac Court, as it is affectionately known. A cold breeze will waft through the air as the unearthly sound of moaning is heard. Thunderous footsteps can also be heard late at night long after the building is empty. Imagination, some may say, right up until the time ghostly activity begins.

Across the street from Mac Court is the Pioneer Cemetery. Listen! No, that's not the wind. It's the mournful sound of bagpipes emanating from the cemetery. Legend has it that if you should see a strange blue glowing light at the cemetery, you know that the ghosts of cemetery residences are out and about and enjoying an evening stroll.

Haunted Elevator at Lane Community College

*W*hy does this elevator seem to have a mind of its own? No matter what button you press, chances are good you will be taken on a trip to the basement. You see, there's a haunted elevator in the Lane Community College according to local lore. It's in the center building, and if you happen to be in the elevator at sunset, you might just hear the mournful cries of a long-ago janitor who fell down the shaft to his death.

"Help me! Help me!"

Salem's Hanging Grounds

Between 1851 and 1859, four men paid the ultimate price for their crimes in this area that was once known as the hanging grounds. This was a time when hangings were still public events, and the public crowded in to witness the execution. What better spot than this that afforded the opportunity for large groups to come and bear witness to the old proverb crime doesn't pay. The area is on the south side of the Pringle Creek and is known as Pringle Park today. As you park your car, think about this: This parking lot is where the gallows once stood—ah, but it's such a lovely place.

And on any day, you'll find people here enjoying the outdoors and the beauty of nature; most of them are unaware of the location's dark past. Because of that past some visitors may feel anxious and out of sorts without realizing why. Some may even catch a glimpse of the forlorn ghost of William Kendall in this area. Even though he protested his innocence and brought in several character witnesses, Kendall was found guilty of the murder of William Hamilton on April 4, 1851. There was little time to prepare for the next world. Kendall's execution date was set for two weeks later, April 18, 1851.

Many felt that Kendall was not guilty and shouldn't have been hanged on such scant evidence. Nonetheless he was. And being the first to legally hang in the new Oregon Territory, he made history. Not that it helped him much; after his death, the county took possession of everything he owned to help defray the cost of housing, feeding, trying, and executing him. How's that for death taxes?

Angered by the way his life ended, the ghostly Kendall haunts the park to this day.

Reed Opera House

The Reed Opera House is one of Salem's oldest buildings. Located in the center of downtown, legend has it that it was built with a million bricks at a cost of $75,000. Built between 1869 and 1870, the building was intended to be used as the home of the Oregon Legislature, Oregon Supreme Court, and Library.

But these plans changed with the next state election. Members of the newly elected state administration backed out of their contract with the builder, Cyrus Adams Reed, and they would not be dissuaded. This left Reed with a problem—what to do with the building. Reed wasn't one to give up so easily. He instructed architect G. W. Rhodes to make some changes. There would be an opera house in the center of the building, space for seven shops on the ground floor, and the remainder of space would be used as the Reed Opera House Hotel.

Under Reed's direction, the opera house quickly became the center of Salem's social life. He was a man ahead of his time. And unlike many of his contemporaries, Reed believed strongly in women's rights. He was the first president of Oregon's Women's Suffrage Association. In 1871 he invited trailblazing feminists Susan B. Anthony and Abigail Scott Duniway, Oregon's women's rights advocate, to the opera house to speak on the issue of women's suffrage.

Reed was also one of Oregon's earliest artists and occasionally helped paint sets for the theater. In 1885, he sold the opera house, and 15 years later it was converted to Salem's first department store. Reed would probably be proud of the opera house today.

Known as The Reed, it contains several shops, restaurants, and a ballroom. Although the opera house has changed hands several times since Reed owned it, he is said to be the ghost that people most often encounter in the building. Looking resplendent in evening attire, the ghostly Reed greets visitors on the second floor just as he might have done a century ago. He doesn't seem to be aware that time has passed. Then again, he may be well aware of the passage of time and merely trying to relive happier times. According to those who've witnessed paranormal activity at The Reed, the second floor is where most of the opera house's ghostly activity takes place

Reed shouldn't suffer from loneliness; he is not the only ghost haunting the opera house. A beautiful woman is also said to make appearances on the second floor. Did she accompany Reed here, or did she come to the opera house unescorted? That's a question worth asking if you should encounter her one evening.

Ghost in a Car

*I*f ghosts can haunt buildings, surely they can haunt cars; we are a nation of car lovers after all. Across the US, there are tales of ghosts in cars, and that can be a scary thing, regardless if the ghost is in the passenger seat or behind the wheel. This story proves that a ghost in a car can also be a nuisance.

It was an especially cold autumn night. The residents of the Royal Court Apartments in Salem were no doubt hoping for a good night's sleep. But that wasn't going to happen tonight. According to the *Capital Journal* of October 15, 1938, someone was parked in a car in the alley near the Royal Court Apartments. And for whatever reason that person kept honking the car's horn. Imagine just drifting off to sleep and being awakened by the blaring of a car horn. It was enough to infuriate the apartment residents who had jobs to get to early the next morning. Some of them swiftly called the police with one demand—make that noise stop.

When a police officer arrived, he saw the problem at once. The car was unoccupied, and what's more, it was locked tight. And yet the horn kept honking and honking. He was no mechanic, but he dutifully looked inside and outside the car; there was nothing more he could do to silence the offending horn. He shivered in the cold night air. He'd done all he could do, and now he was ready to return to the station and its warmth.

The culprit is a ghost, he told himself. But how does one stop a ghost from playing with a car's horn? He had no idea. He began walking from the car. And as he did so, the horn honked at him. He stopped and stared at the car—the horn stopped honking. He took another step and the honking resumed.

Perplexed, he returned to the station. Clearly the solution to the problem was out of his purview. When his supervisor asked him about the honking car, he decided against mentioning a ghost. Instead, he shrugged and replied, "She's still there and she's still tootin'. . . . You figure it out."

Oregon State Prison

*I*t doesn't seem logical that given the freedom to escape, a ghost would choose to stay on at a prison, but they do. Ghost researchers know that prisons are some of the most haunted of locations. Alcatraz in the San Francisco Bay and Philadelphia's Eastern State Prison bear witness to this fact.

There are 14 prison facilities in Oregon; the oldest is the Oregon State Prison in Salem. Established in Portland in 1851, eight years before Oregon attained statehood, the prison was faced with having Front Street run through the middle of the facility. The city of Portland steadfastly refused to reroute the street; thus, the prison remained divided and on either side of Front Street.

But this was an issue that needed to be resolved. Oregon took the easy way out and opted not to deal with the problem at all. Management of the prison would be handed over to a private company. This was a mistake that didn't work out well. Under the management of the private company, the prison saw every inmate escape, proving just how disastrous the plan had been.

The state acquired a new location, and the prison was relocated to the state capital, Salem, in 1866. The history of the Salem facility includes riots and escapes. One of the most famous took place on June 9, 1902, when notorious Harry Tracy and David Merrill shot their way to freedom. In their daring escape, Tracy and Merrill killed three guards, Bailey Tiffany, Thurston Jones, and Frank Ferrell.

Ferrell's brother happened to be Washoe County Sheriff, Charles Ferrell of Reno, Nevada, an excellent tracker. Ferrell eagerly joined the more than a thousand men, lawmen, and volunteers in the pursuit of the ruthless killers. It would take 10 weeks before Tracy and Merrill were found.

In that time, the bloodshed continued, Tracy murdered his friend Merrill and buried him in a shallow grave. While chasing Tracy, members of the posse discovered Merrill's body in Washington and took it back to the prison for burial. Meanwhile lawmen closed in on Tracy, who had nowhere left to run. As they fired at him from all directions, one of the lawmen's bullets found its mark.

Tracy's leg was bleeding badly when they finally came upon him in a Washington wheat field. Even as he exchanged shots with the peace officers, Tracy realized it was all over for him. And he made a decision, he would not be taken alive. To do so meant that he would either rot in prison or be hanged. Tracy put a gun to his head and fired.

Tracy died in Washington, but Washington governor Henry McBride didn't want his state to be stuck with the cost of burying Oregon's criminals, so McBride called Oregon governor, Theodore Geer, to ask if his state was paying for the casket.

"Yes, but only a plain one," Geer replied.

The body of Harry Tracy was prepared for transport and returned to the prison. There Tracy was buried in a grave spread with quick-lime and muriatic acid to destroy the body and any hopes of grave robbers. For several years Tracy and Merrill would lay side by side in the prison cemetery—forgotten.

The prison stopped using this cemetery in 1917. In 1923, the cemetery was paved over and used as a recreation yard. Later, the north guard tower was built here and not surprisingly this is where most of the paranormal activity seems to take place.

A guard who'd worked at the prison for many years told local news reporters that he'd been warned when he first went to work there that strange things happened around the guard tower. Inmates and employees alike have told of ghost sightings and strange noises and occurrences in this area. Two ghosts that resemble Tracy and Merrill have been reported walking together in various locations of the prison, but given that Tracy killed Merrill, it seems unlikely they would have teamed up in the hereafter.

But then, stranger things have happened, I suppose. Other areas of the prison are said to be haunted as well, but the location of the old cemetery is said to be the most active.

Elsinore Theater

*W*hat's in a name? When William Shakespeare wrote *Hamlet* in 1600, he immortalized Denmark's Kronborg Castle as the Castle of Elsinore. The Bard of Avon couldn't have known that three centuries later Salem businessman George Guthrie would use the name *Elsinore* and a castle motif for his lavish theater in Salem. No expense was spared. At its completion, the theater would cost Guthrie a staggering $250,000, which is more than three and half million in today's dollars.

When it opened in 1926, the Elsinore was an immediate success with 1,400 seats, stained glass windows, a big Wurlitzer, and a large stage. Clearly Guthrie was set to bring silent films and top live entertainment to Salem. Three years after the theater opened, the film industry was changed forever with the advent of sound. Through the transition from silent film to talkies, the Elsinore continued entertaining the theatergoing public.

And it did so for nearly a hundred years; however, 64 years after opening, the Elsinore had become a relic of a bygone era. Badly in need of costly repairs and remodeling, it was set to be demolished. Thankfully the Save the Elsinore Committee stepped in and saved the theater. In 1994, the Elsinore was placed on the *National Register of Historic Places*. As it continues on the path Guthrie forged, the theater offers theatrical performances and live music today. And like all theaters, there are the ghosts.

The first and obvious ghost is that of Guthrie himself. He loved his theater. He'd invested a lot of money in it. Why should he leave? Who would take care of the smallest of details? The ghostly Guthrie appears throughout the theater, and they say he is responsible for the stage's ever-present cold spot. Occasionally Guthrie is seen with one of his wives on his arm. This is when he is taking it easy. Stagehands and others have seen the sharp-eyed Guthrie standing nearby and supervising their work—even to the point of breathing down their necks. Admittedly that seems an odd thing for a ghost to do, but the ghostly George Guthrie wants things done his way.

There are no actors and actresses, but there are ghostly children in residence at the Elsinore. A little girl, whose father was an employee of the theater, was playing in the balcony one rainy afternoon when she missed her footing and fell to her death. The ghostly little girl seems unaware that time has passed. She is often seen on the balcony still happily playing.

According to legend, a boy was murdered in the Elsinore men's bathroom back in the day. The ghostly child still haunts the theater in hopes of finding his killer and bringing them to justice. The legend of the ghostly little boy is a twist on the old Bloody Mary legend that promises an appearance by Bloody Mary if you call her name repeatedly in front of a mirror. The Elsinore tale has it that if you stare at the bathroom mirror too long a pair of bloody handprints will slowly appear.

The Elsinore Theater was a nod to Shakespeare and his play *Hamlet,* so it's fitting that the theater is haunted. After all, *Hamlet* is a play in which the plot depends on a ghost.

Dever's Ghost

*U*nless you're interested in the goings-on of Bigfoot (Sasquatch), chances are good that you've never heard of Dever, a small community north of Albany. Today Dever is known as Dever Conner. The small farming community enjoyed some notoriety in the fall of 1960 when teenagers had a brush with Bigfoot at nearby Conser Lake (located on private property today.) A newsworthy event, everyone was out beating the bushes for Bigfoot when he made a brief appearance at the bedroom window of a woman in Dever Conner. Later, measurements were taken of his handprint on the window glass. Bigfoot, it seemed, was larger than the average man. And according to the witness he moved about with great stealth.

As he usually does, the elusive Bigfoot managed to evade hunters and make his way back to his home in the wilderness. But just so you know, Bigfoot is not the only extraordinary visitor to make his way to Dever Conner. In spring 1922, when the little town was still called Dever, Portland newspapers told their readers that a ghost was haunting Linn County. And the specter had taken up residence at a farm in Dever. The ghost was that of a long-ago pioneer who had committed suicide in the house. What's more the newspaper reported, the house might well be for sale. The ghost was still in residence; his antics had frightened the home's owners and sent them fleeing.

But not everyone is fearful of ghosts; some actually like living in their company. A Portland man promptly wrote a letter of inquiry to the owner of the farm. He was interested in the property and wanted to know if it was for sale. The owner was excited at the prospect of a buyer but informed the hopeful buyer that the story was not accurate. The ghostly pioneer had indeed taken his own life, but that had happened at another Dever farm. Thus, if he was haunting any place, it was the other farm.

Besides that, he was sorry to say that after careful consideration, the farm was not for sale, he and his family still lived in their home and liked it; further, it wasn't haunted. And if it were, he said, it would take more than a ghost to scare him and his family off.

Albany

*T*he 11th largest city in Oregon and the county seat of Linn County, Albany is the heart of Oregon. I like Albany. It is a friendly city of less than 60,000 with 30 parks and lots to see and do. One of the many things there is to do is the annual Trolley of Terror tour and walk, which is presented by the Monteith Historical Society and takes place during the Halloween season. And it is fun! If you're like me, you don't visit any city without also checking out its ghosts and history tours. It's a great way to learn more about a place and its ghosts. On the Trolley of Terror tour and walk, you'll hear some interesting tales about the ghosts who reside in Albany.

The following Albany ghost stories were kindly shared with me by the Monteith Historical Society.

Knights of Pythias Lodge

The Knights of Pythias is an international fraternal order founded in 1864. By the 1940s, the popularity of fraternal orders was fading, and membership dwindled. Some lodge buildings were repurposed. The Knights of Pythias Lodge at 230 Lyon St. S. in Albany was built in 1913 in the Italianate style and later converted for use as an apartment building.

Our story begins when a young woman rented a second-floor apartment in the building and settled into her new home. Whatever she might have hoped for, this was not going to be home sweet home. It started one night when she awoke to hear her name being called. Startled she sat up in bed; to her shock, the bed began to shake. An earthquake, she told herself, and jumping from the bed, she ran to the door. The bed stopped shaking. Nothing else in the apartment had been disturbed.

She put it down to a bad dream and went back to bed. Two weeks later she woke in the middle of the night as feelings of dread and apprehension washed over her. Why was she so fearful? Her life was not filled with any problems. She could feel the presence of someone in the apartment with her, and as she tried to coax herself to calm down, she felt hot breath on her face. The sound of heavy breathing was just above her. Trembling, she opened her eyes; she was alone in the apartment.

That was enough. Whatever was in this apartment did not want her here. She stayed awake the rest of the night, waiting for the first light of dawn. When it came, she quickly packed her things and moved out.

Goodwin House

It was sometime in the 1940s and she was the new owner of the Victorian Goodwin House and remodeling it proudly. The house was more than 30 years old and no doubt needed an uplift of sorts. One afternoon she climbed up into the attic for a quick look around and spotted some old bedsprings. These were of no use to her, and she decided they would need to be thrown away. Pushing the bedsprings aside, she stepped around to see what else might be in the dusty attic.

The work was long and tiring, and she was sleeping soundly every night—until the ghost of a long-dead previous owner woke her from a sound sleep.

She gasped when she saw the ghostly old man standing in the doorway of her bedroom. Obviously, the ghost that angrily stared at her was not happy with what she was doing with his house. What had enraged him, she wondered. And then she remembered the bedsprings slated to be thrown away. Okay, she told herself, whatever else I might do to rearrange things, I won't throw the bedsprings away. It's said that they are in the attic to this very day.

People who lived in the house as children have reported seeing ghosts and other strange occurrences. Things were always being moved from one place to the other. One morning a pair of shoes was found across the room from where they'd been placed the night before.

No ghost sightings have been reported in a long time. Still ghosts may be up to their old attention-seeking tricks. Homeowners have told of lamps and other electrical appliances being turned on and off. Strangely enough, most of this activity happens in the doorway area where the angry old man first appeared to the woman who was remodeling the home in the 1940s.

Albany Civic Theater

*J*ust why theaters are so haunted is a question open to discussion. I think this is because of all the emotions, real and feigned, that have been played out on their stages. No doubt other ghost researchers have other equally valid ideas. It is something to ponder during intermission.

The Albany Civic Theater in Albany is more than a hundred years old; that's a lot of actors and actress, performances, and audiences. And like most theaters, there are ghosts on the premises. A ghostly woman made an appearance in the theater in 1989 after a performance of *Gaslight*, the 1938 Victorian thriller. It is a dark play about a man who, with the aid of a household servant, tries to drive his wife insane and collect her money.

After the performance the leading lady, unable to do the customary meet and greet with the public, rushed offstage to keep an appointment. An hour later an actress went backstage to see the leading lady in full costume heading toward the dressing room.

Odd, she thought. She was in such a big hurry to leave and there she is still in costume. Curious, she followed the leading lady into the dressing room. Her costume was hanging on the rack as it always was. How could she have gotten out of that costume so fast? And where was she? There was only one entrance to the dressing room. The actress stopped and stared at the costume. A cold chill ran up her back as she realized that she'd just followed one of the theater's ghosts into the dressing room.

Eugenia Bush

The world is but a canvas to our imagination.
—Henry David Thoreau

*O*ld houses creak and groan, that's a given. Still, they say on quiet evenings in the museum if you listen carefully you will hear the swish of a long taffeta skirt and a woman's soft footfall. This is the ghostly Eugenia Bush, and she is making her way through her former home, the Bush Museum in Salem.

In 1850, Asahel Bush, 26 years of age, left his home in Massachusetts and headed west to Oregon City in the Oregon Territory. There he began publishing the Oregon Statesman newspaper to be the voice of the Democratic Party. A year later, the territorial capital was moved from Oregon City to Salem. Seeing opportunity, Bush packed up and moved his newspaper operations to the new capital as well.

Four years later, Asahel fell in love with and married Eugenia Zieber, the daughter of one of his employees. They would have four children, the youngest of which was his wife's namesake, Eugenia. She is the star of our story.

With the death of his wife in 1863, Bush was left with the responsibility of raising four children and a newspaper to run. He sold the newspaper and co-founded the Ladd and Bush Bank with W. S. Ladd. Although the bank was a success, Ladd wanted out of the banking business and sold his share to Bush. Under Bush's direction the bank became even more successful, making Asahel a wealthy man. A fine new home was in order. The hundred-acre farmstead he and Eugenia bought in 1860 would be the site of the new family mansion.

Bush and his children moved into their new mansion in 1878. Soon the younger Bushes were off to college, getting married, moving on, and building their own lives and successes—except for

Eugenia. Eugenia was never to enjoy a life like that of her siblings. While she was away at college, Eugenia developed a debilitating mental illness that would plague her for the rest of her life. For his youngest child to receive the best medical care available at that time, Bush sent her to a mental institute in Massachusetts. There she would remain until Asahel's death in 1913. Eugenia's sibling, Sally, had never felt right about her sister being confined to an institute so far away from family. As quickly as she could, she brought Eugenia home to the Bush mansion in Salem where she would live until her death in 1932.

The city of Salem acquired the Bush mansion in 1953 after the death of Asahel and Eugenia's last surviving child, Asahel III. Today it is known as the Historical Bush House Museum and, together with its gardens and art galleries, attracts visitors from all over the world. Some of them have encountered the ghostly Eugenia.

Depending on her mood, Eugenia may appear as a child or a young woman. It's said that when she chooses to appear, the ghostly Eugenia plays with favored family items, moving them from one spot to another. Visitors to the Bush Museum have reported hearing footsteps and the voice of a young woman happily calling out to them. There is no call for alarm. It is only Eugenia as she makes her way through the beloved home that was once denied her.

House for Rent in Keizer—Ghosts Included

When I was dead my spirit turned to
seek the most-frequented house
I passed the door, and saw my friends.
— Christina Rossetti

*G*hosts are everywhere, even in charming little houses surrounded by rosebushes, flowering vines, and tall shade trees. But here I've gotten ahead of myself—let's look at Keizer.

Named for Thomas Dove Keizur who brought his family from Missouri to Oregon in 1843, Keizer was settled on the banks of the Willamette River. Yes, there is a spelling discrepancy between its namesake and the city. This happened somewhere along the way from its founding to its officially becoming a city in 1982.

Keizer is a small town, and it was exactly the sort of place the young couple wanted to live in. They were looking for a homey sort of place to rent a quiet little house in a relatively quiet and safe community.

When they saw the house, it seemed like a dream come true. This would be their home. Happily, they both exclaimed, "This is it!"

Certain that they'd found the perfect place, the husband and wife signed a lease agreement and moved their family in. They had no idea of the horror that awaited them. Years later, the young wife still trembled when talking about her experience with the ghost.

> Whatever it was, it was mean and made horrible noises and we never got any sleep—it even pushed me a few times. It was like a dark shadow the few times I saw it. I was never so scared in my whole life. I think it knew I was afraid of it. One of the worst things for me is that nobody believed me when I tried to tell them how bad

it was. They thought I was crazy. We liked all the neighbors. The landlord was nice, the house was so cute. But I knew we couldn't stay there. So we moved out.

Lucky for this family, the ghost chose not to follow them.

Ghost Hill Cellars

The news of their discovery was immediately communicated to the numerous and populous mining camps of Northern California, and people began to move toward the new diggings in considerable numbers.

—*History of Southern Oregon*, A. G. Walling, 1884

In 1851, three years after news of California's Gold Rush brought hundreds of thousands of gold seekers to that state, news of the discovery of gold on Josephine Creek enticed thousands of prospectors to come and try their luck in Oregon. And so they came. Among those who made their way was a bent old man seeking nothing more than his fair share of gold. He kept to himself, working day and night at the water's edge—until the day he discovered the gold nuggets. Now he would have enough gold to ensure a decent life for himself.

Fearing the envy of other prospectors, he didn't say a word about his discovery to anyone. He'd worked hard for his gold, he thought; let the others do the same for theirs. While the others slept, he made his plans. Just before dawn, he quietly packed up, saddled his horse, and headed for Portland. Once he got there, the old man intended to sell his gold and settle into the comfortable existence he'd always dreamed of.

It might have been so, if someone with evil intent hadn't followed him. Worn out from the long journey, the old man laid out his bedroll and drifted off to sleep near the present-day Ghost Hill Cellars at Carlton. Sometime during the night while he slept, the old man was battered to death and robbed of his gold. He would never see Portland again.

Angry at the injustice of it all, legend has it that the ghostly old man stays on, aimlessly roaming the area night after night.

The Frenchman's Lost Ledge

Frère Jacques, Frère Jacques, Dormez-vous?
Dormez-vous?

—Old French Nursery Song

*W*herever gold has been discovered stories are told of lost gold mines and anguished men who lost everything in their pursuit of gold. So intense was their desire for wealth that even death could not deter them. Their ghosts are the stuff of legends. There are tales of Arizona's Lost Dutchman's Mine, California's Lost Pegleg Mine, and Nevada's Lost Breyfogle Mine. To that list I'll add Oregon with the ghost of a Frenchman by the name of Belfils.

The story goes that in 1855 Monsieur Belfils happened upon Josephine Creek. As he drank the icy water, something glittering in the water caught his eye—gold nuggets. He stooped to pick the nuggets up and heard the screams of angry men closing in on him. Fearing for his life, he jumped on his horse and fled. But he would carry a dream of wealth with him for the rest of his days, never forgetting that ledge and its gold nuggets, just waiting for him to scoop them up.

As he grew older and more careless, Belfils talked freely of the ledge at Josephine Creek. Spurred on by his boasts of gold nuggets, other men came to the stream seeking the Frenchman's Lost Ledge. Although some claimed to have done so, no one ever found it—not even Monsieur Belfils himself who tried desperately to retrace the long-ago path that had taken him to Josephine Creek and that ledge. He would spend the rest of his life in his quest.

After his death, people began to talk; perhaps the old Frenchman had been wrong, mad, or nothing more than a liar. Yes, that's all possible. But how do you explain the ghostly man that wanders a certain area of Josephine Creek looking for a ledge that's laden with gold nuggets? Surely, he is the ghostly Monsieur Belfils who appears briefly on the clearest of nights. Perhaps one day someone will wander on that ledge and find Monsieur Belfils' treasure. He doesn't need it; after all, gold nuggets are useless in the hereafter. Even so, the ghostly Belfils continues his search beneath a star strewn sky.

Haunted Holcomb Creek Trestle

*H*ow can a place that seems so innocuous be so haunted? That's a good question and one that is answered when looking at the location's history. The Holcomb Creek Trestle also known as the Dick Road Trestle, spans 1,168 feet and is said to be the longest railroad trestle still in use in the US. Built in 1911 for a now defunct railway line, the trestle near Helvetia is operated by the Portland and Western Railroad.

According to local lore, this wooden railroad trestle is home to a few ghosts. It's said that numerous suicides have happened here; many people have hanged themselves or chosen to jump to their death. Some of them have regretted their decision enough to stay put. Located in a picturesque area of farms and country cabins, the Holcomb Creek Trestle on Dick Road may seem like the least haunted place there is during a daylight drive. But just wait; after dark, the ghosts come out. And the trestle takes on a far different ambiance. Disembodied screams, moans, and sobs have been reported here. Don't be surprised if the apparition of a woman appears in the distance and slowly walks toward you. But don't worry; she means you no harm. Legend has it that the ghostly woman will vanish well before she reaches onlookers. As you watch in the seconds before she dissolves, ask yourself what she wants.

A sordid tale that supposedly took place in the 1960s has a man coaxing his wife and children to the trestle where he slaughtered them all. Satisfied that his family was dead, he then leapt to his death from the trestle and this is where they remain.

Geiser Grand Hotel

Forever is composed of nows.

—Emily Dickinson

*L*et's take a moment and step back in time to a wintry night in 1903. Windswept rain lashes against the windows of the Geiser Grand Hotel. As the night wears on, the temperature drops and the rain turns to snow. Suddenly a hush falls across the lobby as large snowflakes begin falling; before long there will be drifts of snow piled around the hotel.

The sound of laughter draws us to the well-appointed bar where the elderly woman from room 302 is once again holding court in the chair reserved for her. She is stylishly and elegantly attired and wealthy enough so that she commands attention and respect—a raconteur she lifts a glass of sherry aloft and spins tales of her misspent youth, holding rapt every person within earshot. Is there any truth to her tales? That doesn't seem to matter. The old woman knows how to entertain her listeners. A permanent resident of room 302, she is a fixture here at the Geiser Grand Hotel in Baker City and will be for many years to come, even after death has claimed her.

The elderly woman is the specter you're most likely to encounter at the Geiser Grand Hotel in Baker City. And she still wants to be the center of attention. Toward that end, she is known to move guests' personal items around and topple drinks at the bar. And speaking of the bar, woe to anyone that dares to sit in her chair because this will make her a very unhappy ghost indeed. She shows her disdain with a pinch on the ear or slap across the face. You've been warned.

Keeping the ghostly old woman company is a pretty, red-haired dance hall girl and a lovely young woman who wears a lavender velvet gown and has the disconcerting habit of walking through walls. A little girl who runs up and down the stairs and a talkative cowboy who doesn't seem to realize that he's a ghost are also among the other worldly residents of the Geiser Grand.

Employees have encountered an entirely different set of ghosts in the basement and in the hotel kitchen. There is the headless chef—how he got that way no one is quite sure. But don't worry; he's quite friendly to everyone but errant kitchen staff.

The next time you get on the elevator, take a close look at those sharing the ride with you. Some of them may be ghosts because the elevator is rumored to be filled with an entire group of ghosts. They're off to party loudly in a certain room of the hotel.

Some who research and study ghosts will tell you that it's possible to feel ghosts without seeing them and that there is a certain aura about a haunted location. Most will agree that the Geiser Grand Hotel is just such a place.

McMinnville's Mansion at Bayou Golf Club

*B*ryon White was five years old when his family came to Oregon from Oklahoma in a covered wagon. As an adult, White became a chiropractor and settled in McMinnville. He opened the Happy Acres Clinic and Hospital on the grounds where his family mansion was built in 1948. After White's death in 1963 at the age of 70, the clinic and hospital were closed. The following year, his family established the Bayou Golf Course, a regulation nine-hole and a par-three course. And the family mansion was converted to a restaurant.

The golf course and mansion are no longer owned by the White family, but this doesn't mean that the ghost of White isn't still in residence. For years, employees and guests have talked about the ghost they call "Charlie." Some of them believe he is none other than the ghostly White who loved his mansion so much he wants to stay and keep an eye on it.

Charlie may be White, or he may be somebody else. Whoever he was in life, the ghostly Charlie assumes the role of prima donna by speaking to those he likes and ignoring those he doesn't. Don't try to pinpoint just where he may be hanging out. Charlie likes to move around and has been seen or felt in different locations of the building—except for the basement. No one is sure why, but for some reason Charlie will not go anywhere near the basement. Perhaps he knows something we don't.

Five Zero Trees in Oregon City

*O*regon is a progressive state; like many other western states, cannabis is legal. And like grocery stores, department stores, and liquor stores, there are chain dispensary stores throughout Oregon. Our story concerns the Five Zero Trees Craft Cannabis on Main Street in Oregon City. The location is a former pharmacy, and apparently, it's haunted by the ghost of a long-ago pharmacist that has decided to stay in the building. Some eyebrows may be raised at this. But ghosts are everywhere so why not a cannabis dispensary?

Some have said the resident ghost is high from the goodies being dispensed at the shop. Others say the resident ghost is not high—just curious. He often looks over the shoulders of budtenders. But his attention is focused on a tip jar on the counter. The ghostly pharmacist has been known to move the tip jar across the counter. This action was caught on camera as proof of a ghostly presence. It would seem that the ghost only wants more dollars added to that jar.

And I'm sure if you ask him, the ghostly pharmacist will tell you that there is nothing wrong with dropping a dollar or two into the tip jar.

Ermatinger House

*T*he professional paranormal community is a small one. It consists specifically of those who work within the community such as, TV show stars tour guides, historians, writers, speakers, event planners, and presenters. The professional paranormal community is one of the first places I go when writing a book such as this one. Most everyone is willing to share information and other tidbits about the field they love.

It was through paranormal channels that Rocky Smith's name came up. Although he wears many different hats, Rocky is also the director of the popular Oregon Ghost Conference and owner of Haunted Oregon City. As most ghost investigators will tell you, the subject of how one got into the field usually always comes up when discussing ghosts. As we talked, Rocky told me of working at the Ermatinger House and how it led to his becoming involved in the paranormal.

Built in 1845 by Francis Ermatinger, the Ermatinger House in Oregon City is the oldest house in Clackamas County. Although it has been moved twice since it was built, the Ermatinger House played an integral part in Portland's earliest history. The famous coin toss between Francis Pettygrove and Asa Lovejoy took place in the house's parlor during a dinner party. The two men had different ideas as to what the city on their land, the Clearing, would be called. Lovejoy wanted the name Boston and Pettygrove opted for Portland. We know how that went.

According to Rocky Smith the Ermatinger House is haunted.

Most noted is the ghost of an older man who is believed to be a steamboat captain, according to Rocky. He entertained at the house and always sat at the head of the table. He's still there. While he worked at the Ermatinger House, Rocky noticed the chair at the head of the table was pulled out, so he would push it back. Moments later the chair would be pulled out again. This happened several times, although there was no one else in the building. This led Rocky who had been somewhat of a skeptic to take a second look at all things ghostly.

There is a ghostly little girl at the Ermatinger House as well. She is about eight or nine years old and loves ribbons. Rocky told of a coworker who carefully vacuumed the upstairs area one afternoon. After putting the vacuum cleaner back in its closet downstairs, she went back upstairs to find a ribbon in the center of the room. The ribbon, Rocky explained, had been cut from a doll's dress. No one was up there that day. And no one could have done that, but the little ghost girl who loves ribbons.

Guided tours are available on Friday and Saturday at the Ermatinger House. If you plan on visiting, remember to bring a ribbon for the little girl ghost.

Oregon City's Municipal Elevator

*O*regon City is proud of its municipal elevator and rightfully so because the design is unique. Its observation deck may remind you of a flying saucer. Built in 1955 to replace the old elevator, the 130-foot-tall elevator is the only outdoor elevator in the US and one of only four in the world. Connecting the McLoughlin neighborhood and downtown, the elevator was placed on the *National Register of Historic Places* in 2014. If you're expecting that this is an elevator you'll get on and punch buttons, think again. An elevator operator will take you where you're going—on the elevator anyway. And if you're digging in your pocket to pay a fee, forget it; the municipal elevator is free to ride.

For some time now, a little redheaded boy haunts the area where the elevator stands. At sundown, the boy's mother may call him home for dinner, but this child has been at it for decades—he's a ghost. You might not know it to look at him with sunlight glinting in his fiery red hair.

Ask around, no one is sure who this little ghost might have been. He could be a little boy who was killed way back in 1938 when his mother accidentally backed over him in the family driveway with her new car. They say that on particularly wet and rainy nights, the ghostly redhead shrieks in terror.

When I asked Rocky Smith about the ghosts of the elevator, he told me that he has been researching the little boy in hopes of identifying him. Rocky also said that the little redheaded ghost is but one of many children's ghosts that are seen around the elevator. His theory is that the redheaded boy and the other kids died as a result of drinking bad water at Singer Creek.

While we were discussing the elevator, Rocky shared the legend of Sarah Augusta Stevenson Chase who was angry with Oregon City for building the elevator in her front yard. Mrs. Chase took the city of

Oregon City to court to make the city stop building the monstrosity. She lost. Mrs. Chase died on June 30, 1926, but she hasn't given up her fight with Oregon City. She still stands in the observation tower yelling at those who ride the elevator.

A Ghost Caused the Divorce

*T*ill death do us part" is generally part of the marriage vows a couple exchanges. But suppose one or the other spouse decides to continue the marriage even after death? That question and an ex-wife haunted an Oregon City man.

The couple married in 1961, but the marriage was not the happily-ever-after that they'd hoped it might be. A year later, the wife walked out the door, promising never to return. The following year he received word that she had died.

Life moved on and eventually he fell in love anew and remarried. And this is when the ghost of his first wife began reappearing. There was nothing for him to do but go to the Clackamas County Courthouse and file for divorce—from his first wife.

Willamette Heritage Center
(Mission Hill Museum)

The 14 historic buildings at the Willamette Heritage Center are all listed on the *National Register of Historic Places*. And as you might expect, some of the buildings are haunted. But if you've arrived here with your hopes high and your ghost-hunting equipment neatly stowed, you're in for disappointment. Ghost investigations are not permitted at the Willamette Heritage Center. If you should doubt that it is haunted, ask those who've seen the two ghosts, they'll tell you.

> She was dressed in old-fashioned clothing so I thought she was a docent at first. But the more I looked at her I realized I was looking at a ghost.

According to legend, a woman who died when she fell from a nearby bridge is the resident ghost. Keeping her company is a former employee who died here unexpectedly many years ago. Neither ghost acknowledges the other or anyone they happen to encounter; this may indicate that these ghosts are imprinted on their surroundings and are merely repeating a specific occurrence (their unexpected death). And they may be doing this for a very long time.

Laurel Hill on Barlow Road

Came to Laurel Hill This is the worse hill on the
road from the States to Oregon.
> —Absolom Harden in his diary, 1847

*F*irst of all, you won't find any laurels here. Emigrants to the region
mistook rhododendrons for laurels, hence, the name. Many of
those who traversed the Oregon Trail lost their lives along the trail
on Barlow Road. Most of them lie in unmarked graves, forgotten by
time. The lonely grave of one unknown pioneer woman, who had
come westward to Oregon only to die on Barlow Road sometime in
the 1840s, was discovered in 1924 by construction workers building
the Mt. Hood Highway. Her grave was moved to Barlow Road and a
plaque was erected in her honor.

The Oregon Trail stretched 2,170 miles across Missouri, Iowa,
Kansas, Nebraska, Wyoming, and Idaho to Oregon's fertile Willamette Valley. Laid out by explorers Lewis and Clark in 1804 and later
by fur traders in the 1830s, the trail was used by more than 300,000
emigrants from the 1840s to the 1860s. It is estimated that 10 percent of those who traveled the trail did not survive. No doubt this is
why the Oregon Trail is sometimes referred to as the nation's longest graveyard. Not an easy trek, the trail was fraught with danger.
The most dangerous leg of the journey came near their destination
at Laurel Hill on Barlow Road. Even those emigrants who were prepared for the steep hill were shocked at how the wagons had to be
brought down the steep hill so carefully. Once they were at the bottom of the hill, they made camp. Some settled here on the western
side of Mount Hood. Today, it is known as Rhododendron Village
and much of what's left of the old buildings has been restored.

With all the death and heartache that occurred here, there is
no question that the place is haunted. Ghostly activity that's been

reported are sightings of pioneer women who walk through walls, a coughing man, a ghostly old woman who sobs uncontrollably, and children merrily playing and happily unaware that they have been dead for a very long time.

Jacksonville's Haunted Jail

*G*hosts are not a recent phenomenon brought on by the spate of TV shows dedicated to their existence. And just to prove the point, I've included the story of Jacksonville's haunted jail that dates to 1886.

The haunting took place in Jacksonville's second jail that was built in 1875. According to the *Oregon Sentinel* of May 19, 1880, a Chinese man known as Tong was in jail for stealing. Addicted to opium, Tong pleaded with his jailor Captain Caton for the drug. In a move that surely shocks 21st-century jailers, Caton, who wanted to keep his prisoner calm and relaxed, went out to procure the drug for him.

Once Captain Caton was gone, Tong went into action. Desperate to have the truth told, he arranged pieces of paper in symbols on the wall of his cell. He then tore up his bedding and set fire to it. While the fire smoldered, Tong placed a strip of the bedding around his neck and hanged himself from a bar at the window. Try as he might, it was too late for Captain Caton to save him.

With his prisoner dead, Captain Caton curiously stared at the symbols that meant nothing to him. Why, he wondered, had Tong left them there on the wall for him. To find out what they meant, he enlisted the aid of another Chinese man to translate the paper symbols. The young man studied the symbols carefully and then turned to Captain Caton. "He proclaims his innocence of the crime he has been charged with."

Six years passed. In 1886, convicted killer Louis O'Neil happened to be in the same jail, awaiting execution. His last days and nights on Earth were not to be peaceful. A ghost had come into his cell and was harassing him, and he couldn't sleep. The *Oregon Sentinel* of February 13, 1886, carried a story about O'Neil's complaints of sharing a cell with the ghost of a Chinese man. The ghost, O'Neil claimed, was making a nuisance of himself. He moved things around the cell, was creating a terrible noise, and keeping O'Neil awake.

Attesting to the haunting were two guards who'd also heard the ghost. A committee of five citizens came to investigate the haunting and decided it was the ghostly Tong who'd returned to his jail cell. Someone familiar with smudging tried to stop Tong in his ghostly tracks by burning mesquite and cleansing the jail of his energy.

Whatever reasons he'd had for coming back to the jail, Tong disappeared, and the hauntings stopped the moment O'Neil was hanged, thus finally getting some sleep, the following month.

A numerologist might make much of the number three in the following; three years later the jail burned to the ground. Three inmates perished in the flames. A third jail was built on the same spot in 1911. In 1917, jailer Charles H. Basye was mortally wounded at the jail by escaping inmate John Lee Ragsdale who smashed his skull with a five-pound flat iron. When the posse closed in on him, Ragsdale held Basye's stolen gun to his head and fired. He would never have to worry about being incarcerated again.

On June 13, 1917, the *Medford Mail* newspaper carried a story about the irony of both killer and victim lying on slabs within a few feet of one another at the undertakers.

In 1927, Medford became the county seat and a new jail was built there, making the old Jacksonville jail unnecessary. Today the old jail building is home of Art Presence Art Center, which provides a place for local and display artists to present their works, while establishing an art presence in Jacksonville. Surely the creaks and groans occasionally heard in the building are more than just the sounds inherent to old buildings.

Little Minnie

*H*ard to believe today, but Jacksonville was once the largest town north of San Francisco. Gold was the reason. Originally named Table Rock City by James Clugage, Jacksonville was Oregon's first gold rush town. Legend has it that in 1852, John R. Poole and Clugage, made a discovery as they hauled supplies from the Willamette Valley to miners in Sacramento. While watering their mules, they looked into the water and saw gold nuggets. Rather than keep their discovery secret, Clugage contacted newspapers to share the news of gold. Needless to say, this brought thousands of gold seekers into the area.

Four years later, Herman Von Helms arrived from Germany and opened the Table Rock Billiard Saloon. One day in 1862, the 30-year-old Herman met 17-year-old Augusta Englebrecht, and it was love at first site; they were married the next day.

The couple had nine children, but not all of them would live to adulthood. Little Minnie was the couple's youngest daughter and the first to die. Her distraught parents buried her in the front yard of their small home. As he prospered, Herman wanted a larger and finer home for his family. While the mansion was being built on South Orange Street, Minnie's body was removed and reburied at the Jacksonville Cemetery. Even so, the ghostly little Minnie has been seen by other residents of the home over the years. The little specter likes running up and down the stairs.

Apparently unaware that her beloved little Minnie is still in the mansion, the glowing ghost of Augusta appears at the top of the staircase and then wanders through the house sobbing softly for Minnie.

One mystery that's never been solved involves Harry, the youngest Helms' child and last remaining family member to live in Jacksonville. In 1926, Harry Helms suddenly put the house up for sale. After the sale, he packed up and moved—leaving precious family mementoes and heirlooms behind.

Legend of the Lost Cabin

*A*ccording to a story that appeared in September 1900 of the *Oregon Native Son*, a bewhiskered ghost showed up one evening and drew the map that led to the lost cabin and the gold buried beneath it. But here I've skipped ahead. Let's start at the beginning.

With the discovery of gold in Jackson Creek in 1851, thousands of miners came into the region seeking gold. Among them were brothers James and Henry Wilson. As the quest took men further from established settlements, members of certain American Indian tribes became angry at the onslaught of these intruders onto their land.

Fearing war, miners packed up and returned to their homes in town, but not the Wilsons who flatly refused to turn back.

"Goodbye, boys! And good luck to you, but we can't go back. There is gold somewhere yonder behind that smoky line of mountains, and we are going to dig it out. . . . We'll come back rich as kings, boys, or leave our bones to bleach there," James Wilson called after the miners as they mounted their horses and fled the area.

As it turned out, Wilson was partly right. The two brothers discovered gold nuggets, hundreds of them in a nearby stream. As they painstakingly gathered the nuggets, they congratulated each other on their newfound wealth. They were rich as kings, but they would not live long enough to enjoy their gold. Planning to come back for their gold, they buried all of it beneath their cabin and headed back to Jacksonville. Henry died first. James would outlive him by a year. On his deathbed he still vowed to return to the cabin one day and retrieve the gold. Luckily, he had written to a cousin telling him about the gold and the general vicinity of where it could be found. However, he died before he could give explicit details to the cabin's location.

The cousin and a friend set out on the quest for the gold almost immediately.

That first night on the trail, the cousin was visited by a ghost.

> I was somehow conscious of a preter-natural presence. And, looking up, beheld immediately in front of me, a man, or the shadow of a man, tall and muscular, with a brown face and bushy beard. He wore a miner's grey flannel shirt without a coat and had a revolver belted to his side.

Without a word, the ghost kindly drew a map that led the cousin and his friend to the spot where the cabin once stood. Was it the ghostly James offering help from the afterlife? At the cabin, one of the men accidently shot and killed himself and the other went stark raving mad. And the gold?

McCully House Inn

The oldest house in Oregon used as an inn is the McCully House Inn, and it echoes all the charm of a bygone era. Built by Jacksonville's first doctor, John McCully in 1861, McCully House Inn has a past—a ghost. Rumor has it that the doctor himself is the ghost in residence. Apparently, death has caused him to rethink a hasty decision, so he has returned to the house that bears his name.

The McCullys came to the area seeking gold. Like so many others who hoped to become wealthy with a gold discovery, the McCullys were unsuccessful. Dr. McCully hung out a shingle, and Jane sold her baked goods. The McCullys were popular with the townspeople. When a postmaster was needed for Jacksonville, the job went to Dr. McCully who also served on Oregon's last territorial legislature and Oregon's first legislature.

From the outside looking in, the McCullys were a happy and successful young couple with a growing family and a big beautiful new house. But the McCully marriage was in trouble. This secret they kept to themselves. Only the two people involved are privy to the inner workings of a marriage. There isn't much documentation, so historians are left to surmise. Most likely, it was money issues that caused their problems. Still no one knows a marriage's secrets except the two people who share them.

In a time when women had few rights, Dr. McCully decided he couldn't go on. He abandoned his wife Jane and their three children a year after moving into their new home. You'd be wrong if you're thinking that he left Jane empty-handed. He didn't. The good doctor left his wife with more than $7,000 in debt. That would be more than three million of today's dollars and hardly manageable to the average wage earner.

But the resourceful Jane was not one to give up. She baked and sold bread, rented out the bottom floors of her home, and being well-educated, she opened a girl's school. And thus, she was able to keep her home, raise her children, and pay off her husband's debts.

After his desertion, Jane and John McCully would never speak to or see each other again. Who can blame her? And this brings us back to Dr. McCully, who left Jane and the kids to seek gold and to labor at many different jobs. Somewhere along the way he must have had a change of heart. He is the ghost seen at McCully House. Those who've encountered the ghostly McCully say he appears lifelike and there is nothing frightening about him. There he is, sitting in a chair and smiling warmly.

Relax, sip your hot cocoa, and know that there is no reason to be afraid; the ghostly doctor seems to be affable and content. Perhaps he realizes what a foolish thing he did and is hoping to reconnect with Jane. In that endeavor, he is surely wasting his time.

The Green Lady

*I*rish folklore is filled with tales of the banshee, a female ghost who shrieks and screams in warning of the impending death of a family member. Occasionally she will appear as well. Oregon has its own version of the banshee in Jacksonville. One local family's harbinger of death was the beautiful Green Lady ghost. No one knew who she was or where she came from. But according to legend, every member of the family realized what it meant whenever they saw the Green Lady ghost—someone in the family was destined to die in the near future.

The Green Lady only appeared when death was imminent. Unlike the banshee, she never made a sound as she moved slowly through the family home and out into the yard. She had done her job. And she was gone—until the next death.

The Doctor Is in at McLoughlin House

In 1957, the Oregon state legislature named Doctor John McLoughlin the Father of Oregon, a century after his death. This is indeed an honor, considering that he died two years before Oregon attained statehood. By all accounts McLoughlin was a colorful, kind, and generous man who filed a claim for land near the Willamette Falls and founded Oregon City; he was its first mayor and the territory's first coroner. Had he lived, he might have been Oregon's first state governor, but Dr. McLoughlin had powerful and treacherous enemies whose machinations against him ruined his health and sought to take all that he owned.

In the years leading up to his death, he ran afoul of the US government that disputed his claim of ownership of his land and holdings. Not only was his land taken from him, but his home was also. This was a loss that Dr. McLoughlin could not recover from.

Both Dr. McLoughlin and his wife Marguerite were buried at St. John's Catholic Churchyard on Oregon City's Main Street. His headstone read simply:

Dr. John McLoughlin
DIED
Sept. 3, 1857.
Aged
73 Years.
The pioneer and Friend of Oregon.
Also the founder of this City.

But this was not to be Dr. McLoughlin's final resting place. He and Marguerite would be moved three times before they came to rest permanently at their former home, which incidentally was also moved from its original location to save it from demolition.

Whenever you interrupt the eternal sleep of the dead, you are running the risk of a haunting. Maybe they should have known this before they decided to move Dr. John McLoughlin and his wife. From the moment their graves were disturbed, Dr. McLoughlin and Marguerite were said to have returned to their former residence. The ghostly dark figure of McLoughlin has been seen standing at the top of the staircase and crossing into his former bedroom.

Onlookers have also been startled to see the ghostly McLoughlin make his way through the house. There is also the unmistakable aroma of a pipe and that gentle touch on the shoulder or the elbow. But what is a ghostly man without his best friend? A large phantom dog is occasionally seen running through the house. No need to worry about dog hair and allergies, ghostly dogs don't shed.

A former employee of the McLoughlin House told of a strange phenomenon that takes place on September 3, the anniversary of the doctor's death—the glowing painting. At 22 minutes till nine a.m., the sun strikes the painting and its gilded frame in such a way that the face of Dr. McLoughlin glows. It is odd that this only happens on this one day a year, but it does.

Marguerite is also in residence. She is responsible for the rocking chair that seems to move of its own volition. She usually appears at the foot of the stairs and has been known to tap employees on the shoulder. And yet, Marguerite is shy; she will vanish the moment she realizes that someone has seen her.

The Ghosts of the Barclay House

*T*he Barclay House is adjacent to the McLoughlin House. And like its neighbor, there is a ghost or two in residence. Built in 1849, the home of Dr. Forbes and Mrs. Maria Pambrun Barclay was also moved from its original locale to its present site at 719 Center Street in Oregon City. Today the Barclay House serves as a gift shop and as offices of the National Park Service and the McLoughlin Memorial Association. Nonetheless there is always room for ghosts.

Dr. Forbes Barclay was active and well liked in the community; he served in many capacities: mayor, superintendent of schools, and coroner. Neither the doctor's ghost nor that of his wife is often seen at the Barclay House. However, according to legend, there are several ghosts here. One of them is the infant Barclay who died in the house. A little redheaded boy is the ghost most often encountered. According to one story, the redhead is the ghost of a little boy who died in the house many years ago when it stood at its original location.

The baby is never seen but can be heard crying at different times of the day and night. Aside from the redhead is a ghostly black-and-white dog that scampers through the house. Stoop to pet him, and your hand will touch nothing but air. He barks accompaniment as the mischievous redheaded ghost plays one childish prank after another. Staff knows who to blame when anything is missing or goes amiss.

Beside the ghostly dog, the baby, and the redheaded little boy, some of his patients haunt the back of the house. This gives new meaning to house calls.

The Spruce Goose

According to an old saying, necessity is the mother of invention. Howard Hughes must have taken this to heart when he thought of building his Flying Boat. Because of wartime restrictions on the nonmilitary use of steel and aluminum, it was built mostly of birch. The Spruce Goose or Howard Hughes' Flying Boat was meant to transport troops during World War II. It only flew one time. On November 2, 1947, the Hughes H4 Hercules, also known as the Spruce Goose, lifted off with its designer, Hughes at the controls. After a short flight over Long Beach Harbor with journalists aboard, Hughes had proven his point—the plane with the 320-foot wingspan, the largest ever built, could indeed fly. With a shorter wingspan, but a much larger overall capacity, the Russian-made Antonov An-225 snatched the largest title from the Spruce Goose in 2019.

Today Hughes is in residence at the Glenwood Cemetery in Houston, Texas, and his beloved Spruce Goose is housed more than 2,000 miles away at the Evergreen Aviation Museum in McMinnville, separated by time and space. Or are they?

It's well known among ghost enthusiasts that museums and antique stores are haunted. After all, these are the places where the much-loved treasures of dead people are housed. Some of them may cling to their belongings, not wanting to let go so easily. An example of this is the ghostly Hughes who occasionally comes to the Evergreen Aviation Museum for a visit with his beloved Spruce Goose. He doesn't vanish the moment he is spotted. He never says a word or offers an explanation for his presence.

In life he always kept a flight crew at the ready just in case he decided to fly the aircraft one more time. Perhaps in death he isn't as reclusive as he was in life and cannot stay put. That or the fact he's done what countless ghosts have done before him and attached himself to a favored object. Either way there are sightings of the shadowy figure of a man near the Spruce Goose. Odds are it is Howard Hughes.

La Llorona Walks the Banks of the Willamette at Independence

The legend of La Llorona (the weeping woman) is well known throughout Southwest US. La Llorona has been part of Hispanic culture for centuries. Brought to North America by Spanish conquistadors and then to the US by Mexican emigrants, the basic story of La Llorona is that of a ghostly woman who wanders near a body of water seeking her dead children. The tale changes with different storytellers, and there are numerous variants of the story. A popular one has La Llorona drowning her children in a nearby river so that she can be free to go with her lover. Another version has La Llorona killing her children in a violent argument with her husband. And yet in another version, La Llorona is a poor mother whose children wander into the river and drown.

In some of the tales, the ghostly La Llorona is a beautiful young woman. In others, she is a haggard old woman. She always wears white and cries pitifully for her lost children. Some say to encounter the ghostly weeping woman brings bad luck. Others say that merely speaking her name out loud is to court disaster.

In 1988, Pamela Jones collected the La Llorona stories of Hispanic women living in the Rogue River Valley. Her article in *Western Folklore* shares the many different tales of the weeping woman and her lost children that exist in the Mexican culture. The one constant is a mother who has lost her children.

Oregon is a rich culturally diverse state, with a well-established Hispanic community. There are many tales of the ghostly La Llorona. In her book *Haunted Independence Oregon*, author Marilyn Morton tells the story, circa 1950, of a young Hispanic mother whose son is lost to the Willamette River. In a pattern similar to that of La Llorona, the mother's ghost is heard and seen at the river's edge relentlessly calling for her son.

The Ghost at Mangiare Italian Restaurant

A jug of wine, a loaf of bread and thou.

—Edward Fitzgerald

*H*e's got the wine and the bread, if only the poet had put a line in about pasta, glorious pasta.

Mangia! *Mangia*! What is not to like about Italian food—not counting the calories and the carbs of course. The Mangiare Italian Restaurant in Independence is a family restaurant that's been serving up excellent Italian since 2012. Located in the old Sperling Hotel building (circa 1913), the restaurant is proud of every dish and every pizza it serves, including the house-made Tiramisu. Dessert! Yes, now we're talking. It doesn't get much better than a haunted Italian restaurant with a great dessert.

Whatever you order know that it's all local, even down to the wine from the Willamette Valley. The ghostly resident is a local also. And she's not shy about appearing to patrons. Those that don't see her may hear her soft laughter as it echoes through the building. Believed to have been the daughter of a former owner of the Sperling Hotel building, she fell madly in love with a dashing young man and promised to wait for him when he went off to war. But that was never to be. He was killed in the war. When news of his death reached her, the young lady went mad with grief.

Believing that there was nothing more for her in this world, she only wanted to join her lover in death. She climbed to the top of the hotel near the stained glass and jumped headfirst toward the floor. After all these years, the ghostly young lady is still here haunting the old building where she chose to end it all. Legend has it that the blood stains from her terrible death remain to this day. No matter how much they scrub, no one has been able to remove them.

She is no bother. Still, we can hope that one day the young man will return here and take the young lady to a ghostly hideaway for two where they can spend eternity.

May I see the wine list please?

The Ghostly Hector

*O*n December 27, 1929, the *Eugene Register* carried a story titled "The School Is Haunted," about a tiny dog named Hector. Hector died at the hands of a cruel animal abuser in a downtown Eugene alley on Christmas Eve. His lifeless little body was discovered moments after he died and taken to an area near Roosevelt Junior High School where he was buried. But Hector wasn't ready to go. In the next few days, there were reports of a dog's mournful yelps and barking coming from somewhere within the school building.

Police searched the school. While they clearly heard the dog's whining and barking, they could find no evidence of a live dog or of the ghostly Hector. They concluded that Hector had decided the school was the perfect place to spend eternity, especially with the schoolchildren, some of which Hector might have known and liked in life.

As the years passed, the population grew, making a larger Roosevelt Junior High necessary. The new school was built at a different location. If you're curious as to whether Hector is still in residence, you'll be happy to know that the old Roosevelt Junior High is now known as Agate Hall and is located on the campus of the University of Oregon. If you should be at Agate Hall and see Hector, don't be afraid. He's a friendly dog and he doesn't bite.

The newspaper concluded its story with the following line:

> This is the only known instance of a Eugene school building being haunted in recent years.

All I'll add to that is: That was then, and this is now; today many schools in Oregon harbor a ghost or two.

There's a Little House in Lebanon ...

All houses wherein men have lived and died are haunted houses.

—Henry Wadsworth Longfellow

Lebanon is a small town on the eastern edge of the Willamette Valley. Like many of Oregon's cities, Lebanon was named after another town in another state. As you might imagine this town is not noted for its nightlife—unless you're considering ghost activity. It seems that a lot of ghostly goings-on have taken place in Lebanon. Let's begin with a small house that sits on E. Grant Street.

The story first appeared in the national tabloid, *Star*. The *Albany Democrat-Herald* was quick to follow through with an article on May 11, 1982. It's not unusual to see spooky tales of ghosts during the last week of October, but Halloween was five months away. And here was an article that told the plight of a family who'd been living in a haunted house for about a year. Shortly after they'd moved in, the family found a note from the previous owner tacked to the wall, it read: This place is haunted! It didn't take them long to realize the validity of that statement.

The owners knew who to call. They contacted renowned ghost expert and writer Hans Holzer for advice. Holzer suggested a psychic be brought in to communicate with the ghostly young woman. The cost was more than the homeowners were willing to pay. They simply wanted to move on and leave the ghost behind.

And now they were trying to sell the place. Not that the ghost was mean, she was just making a nuisance of herself. Described as a young blonde woman attired in a ghostly white gown, and anywhere from 12 to 20 years old, she liked to make her presence known. She did so by stomping up and down the stairs, playing noisily with toys, and occasionally choosing to appear before the startled family.

Eventually they were successful in selling the house, and the family moved to another residence; hopefully, the ghost stayed put, changed her ways, and didn't tag along.

A White Mule and Fires in the Woodstove

Nature is a haunted house—but art—is a house that
tries to be haunted.

—Emily Dickinson

*A*t one time, ghost stories appeared in newspapers throughout the year and not just during the month of October. On August 30, 1968, the *Lebanon Express* carried a story that told the plight of a family that had once lived in a haunted house in Lebanon. This family had moved into their rental home sometime in the late 1940s. They'd only been in residence a short time when strange things began to happen. Every night around midnight, the family was awakened by the sound of a freight train rumbling through the house. There were no railroad tracks and there was no freight train. They decided it was a ghost playing a trick.

And then the ghostly white mule made an appearance. Try as they may, the moment someone reached out to touch the animal it vanished. This happened again and again. A ghost playing yet another trick, they decided. But it was the fires in the woodstove that finally drove the family from their rented abode.

Fires would suddenly start of their own accord at all hours of the day and night, even when the family was nowhere around. Enough was enough. Frightened of what might happen, the family packed up and moved on. The next family to move in wasn't so lucky. One day while they were all out shopping, a fire started roaring in the woodstove. Flames leapt from the stove and quickly encircled the room. The family returned later that day to find the house and all their belongings had been destroyed in the raging fire.

Who Is This Ghost Anyway?

*T*hose who research such things know that remodeling a building often results in a haunting. Such was the case when a Lebanon couple we'll call Mr. and Mrs. Smith decided to remodel their dwelling. They'd barely begun the project when the haunting began. Imagine waking up in the middle of the night to see a ghostly child standing over your bed. This is what happened to Mr. Smith, as his wife slept soundly beside him. It would not be the last time the ghost appeared to him. Described as a little boy with a bowl-type haircut, the ghost never said a word; he only stared.

One day just as the sun slid into the horizon and darkness overtook Lebanon, Mr. Smith finished mowing the front lawn and stopped to wipe his forehead. As he did so, he absently glanced up at an upstairs window. There was the ghostly little boy gazing back at him. Who was this kid? What did he want? Was there any way they could help him? The Smiths wanted answers. They dug in and did their research even going so far as to interview a previous owner of the house.

No one had any idea who the ghost might be or why he chose to appear only to Mr. Smith and, more importantly, why he was haunting the house. Sometimes there are more questions than answers in the paranormal. This was one of those times.

Bridge of the Gods

Sitting 140 feet above the water, the Bridge of the Gods crosses the Columbia River at Port of Cascade Locks, connecting I-84 in Oregon and SR-14 in Washington. American Indian legend holds that in ancient times, the Great Spirit built a bridge of stone across the Columbia River. With his task finished, the Great Spirit sent his three sons to Earth. But sibling rivalry was taken to new heights when they fell in love with the same woman and began to fight. Their bitter fighting was so intense that the Bridge of the Gods broke apart and fell into the water. Science puts the destruction of the natural land bridge at some time around 1400 CE.

When it was built in 1926, the Bridge of the Gods was named for the legend. My daughter-in-law Peggy has a family story about the bridge. One fog-shrouded day, Peggy's mother, who was about 16 years old, started walking across the bridge toward Washington and home. As she walked, she realized that a taxicab was slowly following her. Halfway across, she stopped. Perhaps someone she knew was in the car. She peered in at the car's backseat and then the front. A chill swept over her. The cab was empty save for the driver—and even in the fog she realized that she didn't recognize him. Whatever he wanted, it wasn't good. In desperation, she crept to the bridge's rail.

It was a long way down. She was a good swimmer, but could she make it? What if he should park the taxi and come toward her? She said a quick prayer and was ready to take her chances by jumping. And then, for whatever reason the taxicab sped off into the fog. Her heart pounding, she practically ran the rest of the way across the bridge.

If she had jumped, chances are she wouldn't have survived. And Bill and I wouldn't have the lovely daughter-in-law that we do. What made the taxi driver drive away? Did he see someone or something

118

standing there beside her on that long-ago foggy afternoon? It's a question that's often been asked.

Some have jumped to their death from the Bridge of the Gods. At least one of them is a transparent gray figure said to walk the bridge on certain nights, forever repeating the last moments of his life when he made a terrible decision.

Central Oregon

Mary Leonard: The Ghost of John Day River

You shall have joy, or you shall have power, said
God; you shall not have both.

          —Ralph Waldo Emerson

*H*ow does one manage to die four times? Adventurer John Day,
for whom the John Day River is named, managed to do so—at
least as far as the written word is concerned. Day's four separate
deaths were duly written and reported until finally even he could
not escape the Grim Reaper. In his honor is the longest undammed
river in Oregon and one of the longest in the US. There's also the
ghost story that has no bearing on Day himself.

Mary Leonard, Oregon's first woman attorney, is the ghost who
haunts a particular riverbank of the John Day. She is driven by her
greed for gold. During Oregon's Gold Rush more than $20 million
worth of gold was mined nearby. When Mary and her unscrupulous
husband got their hands on others' gold, they buried their treasure
planning on retrieving it in the future. They never did. Mary Leonard
has returned from the hereafter to walk the banks of the John Day
River in search of her buried treasure.

Mary and Daniel Leonard, her much older husband, were married on May 18, 1875. Together they operated a hotel near the Dalles
on the banks of the John Day River where the Oregon Trail once
crossed. Rumor has it that the Leonards were nothing but cold-
blooded killers who murdered and robbed many of their clients
for gold and other valuables. But you know what they say about ill-
gotten gains. It's also said that the couple who slays together doesn't
necessarily stay together. After only two years, the Leonard marriage
began to crumble. Gossip was that Mary had a lover on the side,
Nathaniel Lindsay, who also happened to be one of the Leonards'
boarders.

Daniel wasn't stupid; he knew the gossip was true. He filed for divorce accusing Mary of adultery with Lindsay. Mary wasn't stupid either. She countersued. And off to court they went, with charges of wrongdoing between the spouses flying back and forth. The divorce was still going through the court; in the meantime, Daniel was ordered to provide for Mary's maintenance.

Court order, or not, he refused to pay. Mary was outraged and did something she shouldn't have done: She threatened to get even with Daniel and even put it in writing. I have the spirit to get even with you, she wrote. Don't fool with a woman like me.

And then—, someone shot Daniel in the back of the head sending him to his deathbed where he lingered for 12 days. Suspicion naturally fell on Mary and her lover. Both were arrested and accused of assault the next day. When Daniel Leonard succumbed to his injuries, Mary and Lindsay were charged with his murder. After spending 11 months in jail, both Leonard and Lindsay were acquitted of the murder.

Fascinated with the intricacies of the law, Mary had plenty of time to think about her future while in jail. She decided that she should become a lawyer. She studied diligently and passed the bar exam in 1886. Given the anti-feminist climate of the era, she would face an uphill battle in being permitted to become a practicing attorney. She refused to back down, and eventually Mary won the right to practice law in the state of Oregon and became the state's first woman attorney. Seventy-four years later, in 1960 Mercedes Diez blazed another trail by passing the Oregon State Bar to become Oregon's first black woman attorney.

There is much to admire in Mary Leonard's fight for equal rights, but the questions remain. Did Mary and Daniel Leonard murder and rob their boarders? Was Mary guilty of murdering Daniel? The truth will likely never be known. And this could be just one more reason that Mary Leonard's ghost keeps her lonely vigil on the banks of the John Day.

Lillian McElroy Taylor at the Whiteside Theater

Music gives a soul to the universe, wings to the mind,
flight to the imagination and life to everything.

—Plato

*H*er ghostly presence has been seen throughout the theater. She has been dead for decades but hasn't been able to come to terms with that or the fact that the Whiteside Theater in Corvallis no longer needs her services. She never speaks. Occasionally however, there is the nearly imperceptible melodramatic strain of organ music. This is the ghost of Lillian McElroy Taylor, one of those people that has trouble getting past disappointment, and she is playing accompaniment to the tragic turn her life took.

As a young woman Lillian was a beautiful vaudeville performer. Vaudeville was live entertainment and popular with audiences from its inception in the 1890s. Predictably, vaudeville began to fade with the advent of film. Lillian still had her looks and desperately clung to the idea of being an entertainer. As a skilled organist, she saw her chance to stay in an industry she loved. Organ accompaniment was de rigueur for silent film, especially in high-class theaters.

When the elegant Whiteside Theater opened on the evening of November 9, 1922, Lillian was there offering organ accompaniment to the 1915 silent film *The Old Homestead*. The two-manual double touch Wurlitzer had cost a whopping $22,000 and was said to be the largest in the state of Oregon. And Lillian played it magnificently.

The *Corvallis Gazette-Times* reported the opening on November 13, 1922:

> The new Whiteside Theatre was taxed to capacity Friday night, when throngs of people, in spite of the rain,

came out to witness the opening of this magnificent new picture palace. The crowd was so great that in spite of quick work by ticket seller and ushers, the program could not begin until after 7 o'clock. From organ railing to the last row of seats in the gallery, the house was filled, and hundreds stood outside or went away without getting into the first show.

For the next 10 years Lillian lived the dream. By 1932, Hollywood had made another transition; this time from silent to talkie films. Suddenly organ accompaniment was an unnecessary thing of the past. Theater operators looked at their bottom line. Keeping Lillian on the payroll was no longer cost-effective. She was fired. And her world began falling apart. She grew more despondent with each passing day, crying herself to sleep every night.

Lillian faced the realization that she was a relic from a bygone era—a jobless relic with a philandering husband. It couldn't get much worse than that. Or could it? Adding insult to injury, Byron, her abusive husband was two-timing her with a younger woman. There was nothing she could do. And when she thought about it, Lillian realized there was nothing but a hopelessly unhappy future before her.

On the night of February 22, 1932, Lillian's daughter and her sister were visiting at her home. Without stopping to think of the consequences, Lillian locked her bedroom door and put a gun to the back of her sleeping husband's head. Then she pulled the trigger, putting an end to his two-timing.

Satisfied that he was gone, she put the gun to her breast and pulled the trigger again. Awakened by the noise, her relatives pounded on the locked door.

"Lillian, open the door at once!" her sister shouted.

"Mother, please open the door," her daughter begged.

Mortally wounded, Lillian didn't have the strength to do so. Police officers arrived a half-hour later and broke down the bedroom door. Lillian was dead on the bedroom floor; a few feet away the philandering Byron was dead in his bed. It was the end to her cheating husband and all her troubles, but Lillian hadn't thought things through.

If she thought she would be escaping the misery that was her life, she must have been disappointed to realize the only place she has gone is back to her beloved Whiteside Theater.

Local lore holds that the ghostly Lillian remains at the Whiteside Theater, even after fires, remodeling, and time.

Oregon State University

$\mathcal{E}$very university in the US probably has a ghost story or two associated with it. The Oregon State University in Corvallis has several. Let's start with Sackett Hall. Built in 1948 as a women's dormitory, Sackett Hall is one of the oldest dorms still in use today. The ghostly resident here is known as Brandy. According to legend, Brandy was murdered in the building sometime in the 1970s by notorious serial killer Ted Bundy who admitted to killing at least 30 people.

Although Bundy faced justice when he was executed in Florida on January 24, 1989, Brandy remains an angry and unhappy ghost. She resides in the basement of Sackett Hall and enjoys wreaking havoc throughout the building. She shrieks at all hours of the night, causes icy drafts, and unlike the dog that ate the homework, she likes to misplace books and other essential study items.

Ida Kidder was the university's first librarian; as such she lived in Waldo Hall from 1908 until her death in 1920. Apparently, she's still content to stay on the fourth floor where she once lived. Built in 1907, as a women's residence, Waldo Hall is used today as offices. Ida must not be aware of this as she keeps watch over her former home.

She is a loner and in no mood to discuss the Dewey Decimal System. Whenever she is spotted in the hallways, Ida quickly turns and walks through the nearest wall. Still she likes keeping an eye on the campus. Some have reported seeing Kidder's apparition staring down at them from the fourth floor late at night.

Built in 1949, Dearborn Hall was the site of the university electrical engineering program. A student, or so the story goes, was electrocuted in one of the classrooms in Dearborn Hall. His handprints remain on the wall to this day. And his heart-wrenching screams echo through the old building on certain nights.

Over in Langton Hall, there's a ghostly swimmer who occasionally takes a dip in the pool. The ghost of a long-ago student who drowned here, the swimmer doesn't bother anyone. But do expect the water to be icy cold whenever he is swimming. Built in 1915 as the men's gymnasium, it was renamed Langton Hall in the early 1970s and is used for physical education as part of the biological and population health sciences school.

It's said that Benton Hall is the most haunted location on campus. This is home of the College of Liberal Arts' music program, and that might explain the ghostly woman who has been heard singing throughout Benton Hall. She has a lilting soprano voice, but it doesn't make up for the other ghost here at Benton Hall. He, or she, doesn't want to entertain with a ghostly repertoire. This ghost likes to play tricks on the custodial staff. Brooms, mops, and vacuum cleaners have all been moved or have totally disappeared, much to the annoyance of staff.

Cheldelin Middle School

Some people are workaholics; they love their job so much that they hate to leave it behind even on the weekend. So here is yet another story of an employee who enjoyed his job so much that he continues to work—even in the hereafter. The story goes that one afternoon a janitor at Cheldelin Middle School in Corvallis suffered a heart attack in the gym. By the time emergency medical technicians arrived, it was too late for lifesaving measures.

Fast-forward a month; the janitor was back on the job, pushing a broom and whistling various old show tunes. He's a ghost, you say. Well, yes, he is. But he's making good use of his time, seeing that the school is in shipshape. Hear the sound of jangling keys? That's also the ghostly janitor. He has lots of rooms to clean.

Dawson House Lodge

*T*he Dawson House Lodge in Chemult has been haunted for decades. At least that's what some of the guests have said after spending some time at the lodge. With the opening of the new Highway 97, more travelers would be coming this way, and they would need a place to stay, as would railroad and highway workers. To accommodate all of them, Dick Dawson built his 12-room Hotel Chemult in 1929. Three years later, Dawson sold the hotel to Mr. and Mrs. Hugh Porter.

Somewhere along the way, ghosts took up residence. Some of them are seen and not heard. One of these would be the ghost who tries to climb into bed with men who are staying alone. If you should hear someone laughing uproariously at the Dawson House Lodge, it doesn't mean that a good joke has been shared. Disembodied laughter is a common ghostly occurrence. Nobody seems to know what's so funny or just why this ghost is laughing. While you're listening for ghostly laughter you may as well be aware of the large ghost canine who wanders about the lodge; they say he doesn't bite.

Jack London's Still Writing
at Wolf Creek Inn

You can't wait for inspiration. You have to go after
it with a club.

—Jack London

*D*o writers ever stop writing? There are some editors who might
answer no to that question. But what if said writer were a
ghost? That could make a difference—or not, especially if that writer
happened to be Jack London. London's writing career was not a long
one, spanning 17 years from late in the 19th century to early in the
20th century. In that time, he wrote more than 50 books. He is best
known for his adventure novels *Call of the Wild* and *White Fang*. He
wrote many more, including short stories.

While finishing *Valley of the Moon*, London stayed at Wolf Creek
Inn. Wolf Creek Inn was a favorite place, and he spent as much
time here as possible. Some believe he has never left. It's easy to see
where he may have believed this was possible. In *Call of the Wild*,
the main character is Buck the dog who becomes a ghost—a ghost
who returns to avenge a wrong.

Local businessman Henry Smith had the Wolf Creek Tavern built
as a stagecoach stop on the Applegate Trail in 1883. Twenty or so
miles from the Rogue River, Wolf Creek Inn is the oldest continuously operating hotel in Oregon and the Pacific Northwest. Former
notable guests include John Wayne, President Rutherford B. Hayes,
Clark Gable, Orson Wells, and Sinclair Lewis.

Today Wolf Creek Inn offers nine rooms, and many of them
come with a ghost—or two. As much as you might want to stay in
Jack London's room, that's not going to happen. London's room is
preserved much as it was the last time he stayed here at the inn. But
you're free to take a peek at the room. And who knows, while doing

so you just might encounter the ghostly London himself. Guests have reported seeing him standing in the room and the hallway. Some have even heard his voice.

My question is, if he is a writer with a deadline why doesn't anyone ever hear the clacking of typewriter keys or see the author bent over a desk, pondering his next sentence?

There are other ghosts and paranormal happenings at Wolf Creek Inn. Some of them can get mischievous by moving furniture around and misplacing cooking utensils in the kitchen. And the piano, not a player piano, yet, occasionally a ghostly pianist will sit down at the old piano in the parlor and play a cheerful melody.

Pendleton Center for the Arts

In the early 1900s, steel tycoon Andrew Carnegie put his millions to work for the public good by funding thousands of libraries across the country. Using funds from Carnegie's good deed, the Umatilla County Library was built in Pendleton in 1916. Later it would be called the Pendleton Public Library. Today the building serves as the Pendleton Center for the Arts. But don't share that information with the ghost. She still thinks of it as a library.

On October 11, 1947, daylight was fading as the last patrons walked out the door, books in hand. Wishing them good evening, the assistant librarian, Ruth Cochran, locked the door behind them. As she began turning lights off and closing the library, she felt a sharp twinge of pain—a headache. At 52 she was used to occasional aches and pains. This was different. She sat down and waited for the headache to subside. It didn't. She slowly made her way down to the basement to rest.

Cochran was discovered the next morning and rushed to the hospital. She died the following afternoon. That's the story. Now for the legend: The assistant librarian was so distraught when her lover abandoned her that she crept down into the basement and swallowed lye. She was dead before she hit the floor.

Her ghost remains in the building to this day—and night. On quiet evenings, the sounds of her footsteps can be heard as they echo across the floor. She's also been spotted throughout the building and occasionally staring out the window.

Morrow County Courthouse

Built between 1902 and 1903, at a cost of $56,900, the Morrow County Courthouse in Heppner is an imposing structure. It is also one of the oldest continuously operating courthouses in the state of Oregon. In 1985, the courthouse was listed in the *National Register of Historic Places*. And it's haunted.

Local legend holds that there may be a lot of ghosts wandering the halls of the courthouse—24/7 of them by some accounts. Three months after the courthouse was opened, disaster struck. In her book *Calamity: The Heppner Flood of 1903*, author Joann Green Byrd says it was the deadliest natural disaster in Oregon's history. It is the second-deadliest flash flood in the US according to Christopher Burt and Mark Stroud in their book, *Extreme Weather*.

June 14, 1903 was another hot dry day in Heppner and everyone in the small farming community of 1,400 was hoping for rain. By early afternoon it looked as if rain may be coming; toward the southwest a storm was brewing. Around five in the evening, a thunderstorm roared across the sky and heavy rain began falling. Within minutes, the rain turned to hail and beat down on roofs and buildings, causing a thunderous racket. Willow Creek was swollen and overflowing; suddenly a wall of water swept through the town of Heppner, ripping buildings apart and claiming the lives of 247 people, one-fourth of Heppner's population.

Reporting on the storm the *Heppner Gazette* stated:

> Without a second's warning, a leaping, foaming wall of water, 40 feet in height, struck Heppner at about 5 o'clock Sunday afternoon, sweeping everything before it and leaving only death and destruction in its wake.

Three days later on June 17, 1903, the *Oregonian* reported:

Houses crushed and telescoped beyond recognition, buildings twisted from their foundations, deposited in streets or on alien property, one-fourth, or one-half, or one mile away; household goods strewn in every direction in reeking mud; trees two feet in diameter uprooted and woven in impeded drift into all kinds of awful fantastic shapes, bodies of men and horses and cattle and pigs all cast in indiscriminate ruin—such is Heppner of today.

The courthouse basement was offered as shelter for those who had lost family and friends, those whose homes were destroyed in the flood, and those who'd lost everything. Imagine the feelings of desolation and heartbreak that were being experienced in that basement in the days and nights that followed. Not everyone who came to the courthouse basement would survive. Perhaps some of their ghosts are still here in Heppner in the stately old courthouse.

Disembodied voices, footsteps, and unexplained noises are offered as evidence. But that same evidence could apply if the ghosts happened to be those of the murderers and criminals who stood trial in the courtroom upstairs.

Because of the unexpected devastation and death the flood brought, there are those who believe that Heppner is haunted throughout. One place people point to as haunted is Murray's Drug located in the Roberts Building. It was built in 1901 and was one of Heppner's few buildings to withstand the 1903 flood. Because few buildings remained, the bodies of flood victims were brought to the Roberts Building for identification. Some locals believe the building is home to a couple of ghosts who lurk about, mischievously calling people by name and lowering the temperature as they move about.

Underground Pendleton

*P*endleton was once notorious for its four-block area of 32 saloons and 18 brothels. Today a bronze statue to Pendleton's famously infamous madam, Stella Darby, stands on Main Street outside the Medernach Building where her brothel, The Cozy Rooms, once stood. Discreetly entering and exiting Stella's Cozy Rooms and other illicit businesses was assured through secret tunnel entrances. And as business expanded, so did the city beneath a city, which was a secret that wasn't discovered until the mid-1980s.

Underground Pendleton dates to a time in the state's history when the Chinese were so discriminated against that they feared for their safety. With ordinances that forbade them from being on the streets after dark, the Chinese needed a safe place to live. As refuge, they took up residence in the tunnel system they'd helped to build. Thus, they created their own city beneath the city. They were free to move about and live free of the racism and fear that pervaded the US at that time.

Brothels, saloons, and opium dens flourished in Pendleton's underground city. Over time, others came to live in the city beneath Pendleton. Local lore has it that some of their ghosts still reside here in the underground tunnels.

Ghosts at the Deschutes Historical Museum

A modern marvel when it was built in 1914, the Reid School featured 10 classrooms, indoor toilets, an auditorium, and a central heating system. For the next 63 years, the school served the children of Bend. In 1977, the school was closed, and the Deschutes Historical Museum was established in the old building. Somewhere along the way, a ghostly gent took up residence in the museum.

No one is certain, but the general consensus is that the ghost is that of George Brosterhous, who, along with his brother Ed, was one of the school's original contractors. The unfortunate George Brosterhous fell to his death on June 3, 1914, at the building. Depending on which story you believe, he either fell from an open stairway on the third floor or was standing on the roof when he lost his footing and fell. Either way, his injuries were fatal. But not to worry, he has decided to stay put. The ghostly George is blamed for making all sorts of mischief in the museum. From moving items so that they are never seen again to a plethora of strange noises and occasionally appearing to the unsuspecting, George is on it.

But George also has his friendly side. He has been known to help researchers find just the item they are looking for. A ghost that will help with research can't be all bad.

But there is another ghost on the premises as well. Those who've seen her say she is a schoolgirl of about seven years old and appears to be wearing clothing in the style of the early 20th century. She turns water faucets on and off and flushes the toilets in the women's bathroom at all hours of the night. The ghostly little girl can sometimes be heard giggling to herself. One thing seems to be certain. She and George like it here at the museum and show no inclination of leaving. And as any ghost researcher will tell you, if a ghost has decided to stay on, there really isn't much you can do to evict them.

Little Theater on the Bay

By now you've probably realized that there are a lot of haunted theaters in Oregon. Oregonians are theatergoers. If it isn't ghostly actors and actresses staying on at the theater some members of the audience have decided to remain after the curtain goes down as well. The Little Theater on the Bay in North Bend is at the Liberty Theater. Formed in 1947 by a group of actors that wanted to do live radio plays, the little theater is home to a ghost that is believed to be the mother of two small children who tag along with her.

Her clothing and that of the children is from an era well before the 1940s. Legend has it that she died here in the bathroom at the theater, but the details of her death are sketchy. One thing that is clear is her presence and the fact that she refuses to leave.

Franz Edmund Creffield

Love is a misunderstanding between two fools.
—Oscar Wilde

*F*air warning: This one is a weird and sordid little tale that may leave you aghast, especially because it actually happened.

Our story begins with the dawning of the 20th century; it takes place in the small city of Corvallis on the west bank of the Willamette River. Less than 2,000 people lived in Corvallis. The small farming community may have seemed ideal to German immigrant Franz Edmund Creffield who came here in 1903.

A self-righteous religious man, who had parted ways with the Salvation Army, Creffield was not someone that others might find charming, and certainly no one would have called him handsome. But he was gifted with an abundance of charisma that drew people to him, especially women. And, thus, the charismatic Creffield founded the religious movement he called the Bride of Christ Church. Although the women were impressed with him and his teachings, the men were not. And this would cause many disagreements between husbands and their wives. One by one, men dropped out of Creffield's church, leaving a congregation of mostly women.

Creffield and his followers were considered odd and referred to as Holy Rollers. This didn't matter to the sanctimonious Creffield. For much like George du Maurier's Svengali in the 1894 novel *Trilby*, Creffield hypnotically persuaded women to mindlessly follow him, regardless of what their husbands, brothers, and fathers might think or say. When wives came to him worried about what their husbands thought, they were told it didn't matter what they thought because marriage, Creffield assured them, was unnecessary.

Up until this time women had been raised to believe that marriage was the best a woman could hope for in her life. And once married, a woman would be totally dependent on her husband. The husband would make all the decisions and the wife was not to question them. So here Creffield offered a refreshing viewpoint; women had never been told that marriage was unnecessary. Nor had they been shown the freedom to disobey husbands by forgoing all the encumbrances and duties they endured as women. Men despised Creffield for what he was teaching their wives, sisters, and mothers.

Because of his involvement with married women and underage girls, Creffield was accused of adultery, debauchery, and other such crimes. To avoid being arrested and put in jail, he led his followers to other parts of Oregon. In 1904, a group of vigilantes found Creffield's house, broke through the door, and punished him with tarring and feathering. Yes, it is as bad as it sounds; the procedure involved pouring hot tar on the victim's body and throwing feathers at them so that the feathers would stick to the tar. Once Creffield was sufficiently punished, the vigilantes ordered him to leave town at once. Instead, he got married and wisely stayed on the down low.

His most ardent followers were sent to the Oregon State Insane Asylum. The law hunted Creffield, who was officially charged with the crime of adultery for his affair with a relative of his wife's. Eventually lawmen caught up with him, and while in jail and awaiting trial, Creffield didn't help his cause when he told a reporter from the *Oregon Daily Journal*:

> I am now Joshua, high priest and at some future time, will become Elijah, the restorer. My work is to lead the 13 tribes of Israel back to Jerusalem, where the restoration of all things will take place and the millennium will dawn on earth. I have a mighty work to accomplish. That work I will accomplish as God directs.

On the witness stand, O. V. Hurt, Creffield's father-in-law testified of Creffield's followers, "They did whatever he said. They were dead to all human sympathies. They let their children, their husbands, and their parents go uncared for and without a kind thought or word."

He ended his testimony by calling Creffield a human vampire.

Creffield might have held sway over his followers, but the judge and the jury, made up of men, were not so easily impressed. He was found guilty and sent to prison for two years. Upon his release for good behavior 17 months later, Creffield announced that he had brought his wrath down on San Francisco with the devastating 1906 earthquake. He now put a curse and called for an earthquake to rock Corvallis. To avoid the impending disaster, he and his flock would move to Waldport and then inland.

Finally released from the insane asylum, his followers believed anything he told them. Whatever he hoped to achieve, Creffield soon realized that Oregon was no longer safe for him. Too many men were angry at the ease in which he'd sexually manipulated their wives, daughters, and sisters. Attempts had already been made on his life. Creffield and his wife packed up and went to Seattle.

But there is no escaping one's fate. George Mitchell, the brother of Creffield's 16-year-old lover, had been looking for him for a long time. When he finally found him, walking on a downtown Seattle street, Mitchell sauntered up to him and calmly shot him in the back of the head. Mrs. Creffield and several witnesses recoiled in horror as Creffield dropped to the sidewalk. Mitchell calmly waited for the police to come and arrest him.

After a sensational trial, Mitchell was found not guilty and released from jail. The celebration was short-lived. Just as the man he'd shot and killed could not escape his fate, there was no escape for George Mitchell. His own flesh and blood killed him. Angry that he'd murdered her lover, Mitchell's sister shot and killed her brother, a crime for which she would spend several years at the state insane asylum. When she was finally released in 1914, she committed suicide. Creffield's widow then killed herself as well.

So now we come to the northbound OR 99W bridge over Mary's River at Corvallis. The historic truss bridge was built decades after Creffield's death. It is near the spot where Franz Edmund Creffield lived. It is also where you'll find the ghostly Franz Edmund Creffield. Angry at the wrong done to him, he maliciously lingers, cursing, and causing mishaps and trouble on the bridge. Corvallis, he believes, is the place that treated him so unfairly, ultimately causing his downfall. How long will he remain here? He could be here another week, or he could be there forever.

The Farmer Almost Takes a Wife

Fossil is a small city. With less than 500 residents, that's an under-statement. Fossil's claim to fame is its fossils for which it was named in 1876 by Thomas Benton Hoover. It was at Hoover's ranch that Fossil's post office was first established. The city was incorporated in 1891, and today Fossil is the state of Oregon's only public fossil field. Access to the field will cost you a small fee, but hey think of all those fossils of dinosaurs and other ancient creatures and plants.

Our story is not as old as dinosaurs. It opens around the turn of the 20th century. A farmer and a wealthy young woman fell in love. Her family didn't think she would be happy leading such a life of drudgery; they wanted much more for her than the life of a farmer's wife. No matter how she begged them to reconsider, her parents were adamant. When it became clear that her parents were not going to relent, the young woman jumped to her death from the third floor of a Fossil bed and breakfast.

The distraught farmer blamed himself for her death. So did the people of Fossil. The next day the farmer hanged himself in a tree near the bed and breakfast. A variation of this story has the people of Fossil angrily lynching the farmer. The two lovers were dead and perhaps rejoined in the afterlife.

Let's fast forward to the 21st century, and the Bridge Creek Flora Inn in Fossil. The story of the star-crossed lovers has survived. The sorrowful young woman is often seen peering out from a third-floor window of the bed and breakfast. The specter of her lover is some-times seen hanging in a tree. People who have stayed at the Bridge Creek Flora Inn have reported encounters with the young woman who wears a pale pink dress and is followed by the aroma of rose perfume and a cold chill. Perhaps the lovers have not reconnected in the afterlife after all.

If you would like to visit Fossil and the ghostly young woman at the Bridge Creek Flora Inn know this: The inn has either changed its name or closed its doors. Sad as this is, it is not a total loss. The tree with the specter of the farmer is still standing, there are other hotels and motels in Fossil, and there is that fossil field with all those dinosaur fossils, just waiting to be discovered.

Sparrow Bakery

*L*et them eat cake" is a statement attributed to France's ill-fated queen, Marie Antoinette. Some historians argue that she was misquoted. And perhaps she was. I agree with her sentiment and would take it a step further—forget the carbs today. Let's eat fresh bread, pastries, scones, cake, and croissants.

Rumor has it that a ghost with a sweet tooth and an appreciation of the finer things in the afterlife, has taken up residence at the Sparrow Bakery in the old Iron Works Art District Bend. In addition to an extensive sandwich, soup, and salad menu, there are beignets, croissants, and let's not forget the aroma of freshly baked bread—lather on some jam and you're good to go. Can you blame the ghostly gent for wanting to hang out here? I mean on a list of 10 best places to haunt surely a bakery would be at the top of the list.

The Sparrow Bakery Northwest is housed in an old brick building that was built in 1920 for use as the payroll office for Bend's Iron Works. Granted old buildings creak and moan, but they don't roar with laughter like the ghost at Sparrow often does. Nor do they open and close doors and announce themselves with noisy footsteps. And, of course, they don't care about croissants, scones, and other heavenly goodies. The resident ghost here enjoys misplacing things or moving them around. He's the friendly sort. But just to be on the safe side, a scone is occasionally left for the ghost.

The Ghost Light at Tower Theater

A Whistling Woman and a Crowing Hen always
come to a very bad end.

—An old Irish proverb

*M*an, woman, or crowing hen, whatever you do, don't whistle in
a theater. It's considered bad luck. Just so you know, theater
people are superstitious. None of them would dare to bring peacock
feathers, a mirror, or real money onstage. None would wish another
performer good luck before a performance. Neither would any of
them ever say the name *Macbeth* aloud while in the theater if the
play was not being performed there. The play is said to have been
cursed by the Bard of Avon himself. So in an abundance of caution,
it is referred to as the *Scottish Play*. Thus, the doom that might follow
the faux pas is averted.

That's the theater for you. But there's another thing about theaters, they're all haunted. And it's considered good luck to keep a
seat open and available for the resident ghost. Yes, ghosts enjoy theater. Big or small, new or old—have you ever heard of a theater that
didn't have at least one ghost in residence? Neither have I. And that
brings us to the Tower Theater in Bend.

The Tower Theater was built in 1940, and for the next 60 years,
a lot of great and not so great films and live events took place there.
In 2004, the theater was revamped as a live performance theater
and this is where the ghost makes their entrance. Plenty of people
have seen them. But no one knows who they are, this ghostly couple
that sits in the back row of the theater, taking it all in until someone becomes aware of them. That's when they move on. There is
another ghost who flits around the theater in costume.

Who is she? No one seems to know. Does it matter? All that
applause is music to her ears. Perhaps she should take another curtain call—and another—and another.

Like most other theaters across the country, when the Tower Theater is still and everyone has gone for the evening, the ghost light is turned on and shining brightly. Why is that? There are some explanations. One is of course for safety purposes. Anyone walking around after the lights have been turned off is guaranteed not to trip or fall over something unexpected. And that makes sense to me.

But there is another explanation that involves ghosts. The ghost light, it's said, is to aid resident ghosts who, like the living, prefer not to stumble around in total darkness. Why else would they call it a ghost light?

Northern Oregon

Fort Clatsop

I wonder how many times ghosts are ignored and forgotten simply because they are mistaken for docents. That's what happens at Fort Clatsop. Dressed in attire of two centuries ago, a ghostly man wanders this area. And yes, those who see him often assume he's a docent going about his work. Right up until they speak to him.

Fort Clatsop is an old place. Lewis and Clark's Corp of Discovery expedition took the advice of the local Clatsop tribe by choosing this location at the mouth of the Columbia River for their winter encampment. They called it Fort Clatsop in honor of the local American Indians who had helped them in their work. They settled in and prepared to spend the winter of 1805–1806.

With spring, they prepared to leave the area and head back to St. Louis. In gratitude for all he and his people had done for them, Lewis and Clark gifted the fort to Coboway, the Chief of the Clatsops. Time and the region's dampness have long since destroyed the original buildings; still, it is historically significant. Fort Clatsop is a small place, an old place, and a haunted place.

And this brings us back to the countless people who have shared similar tales of stopping to chat with a docent only to discover that he is not a docent at all, and he is certainly not of this world. A woman told of encountering the ghostly docent one rainy afternoon.

> My husband and I were getting drenched and running for the car. There this docent was, standing in the pouring rain without an umbrella or a care in the world.
>
> "No wonder, Lewis and Clark left this area," my husband laughed as we got closer to him.
>
> He didn't even acknowledge us. Just stared straight ahead; now the really weird thing was, he wasn't

getting wet. We were soaked. He wasn't. That's when I knew. He was a ghost. It gave me a chill, I can tell you that much.

Cursed Treasure and the Ghost
of an Angry Sea Captain

There is no history, only fictions of varying degrees
of plausibility.

—Voltaire

In one of his many books on myths and legends, writer Charles
Montgomery Skinner offered a story of buried treasure that took
place around Columbia City in 1841.

Although he'd tried to keep it a secret from them, the captain
of a Spanish ship realized that his crew of rowdies had discovered
there was valuable cargo aboard. Unaware of the men's plotting,
the captain didn't sense danger until it was too late. Near Columbia
City, the crew slaughtered him and took the valuables ashore where
they hastily buried them.

As agreed, the men returned to the spot a few years later. They
would finally dig up and divvy their treasure. Everything had
changed. To their dismay, none of them could remember exactly
where the treasure had been buried. Disappointed and empty-
handed they went back to their ship.

That might have been the end, except for something that happened on the other side of the country in Hydesville, New York. Two
young girls began communicating with the dead. The Fox sisters
captivated those who were eager to communicate with people in the
afterlife and gave rise to the Spiritualist religion. Men and women
who were able to talk with the dead called themselves *mediums*. A
medium and a member of the Spiritualist Church, in Columbia City
received a message telling exactly where the treasure was buried.
After she shared her information, a group of friends went out digging for the treasure. But they made a grave mistake; as they dug
their way through the location they all suddenly fell dead.

Years later another group attempted to unearth the buried treasure. While digging, they came across a dozen or so skeletons. One man was said to have become stark raving mad at the sight. Apparently, the ghost of the murdered captain keeps the buried treasure from anyone who might get too close, agreeing with the words of playwright/poet Sir Walter Scott, "revenge, the sweetest morsel to the mouth that ever was cooked in hell."

Dammasch State Hospital

*T*he Dammasch State Hospital in Wilsonville no longer exists. However, it opened in 1961 and was closed 30 years later in 1995. Named after Dr. Ferdinand Dammasch, who died in 1955, the hospital served as an asylum, a mental hospital, and an educational facility. During its period of operation Dammasch State Hospital saw more than 20 deaths. Some were accidental, and others were from natural causes.

After the hospital was closed, there were reports of a ghostly woman walking among the dilapidated buildings. She was not the only ghost that roamed the abandoned site and the grounds. Ghost sightings and disembodied voices were whispered about, and a few paranormal investigations took place here.

Eventually after much discussion and disagreement as to what the site should be used for, the Villebois Wilsonville master community was built on the site. The houses are beautiful and new and what an absolutely outstanding place to call home. And yet I wonder if the lonely ghosts of the state hospital still roam.

Scaponia Park

Scappoose is a small Portland bedroom community located about 20 miles north of the city. Many visitors to Scappoose come for its park—Scaponia Park. A small seven-acre wooded park with 12 campsites, hiking trails, and Gunners and Floaters lakes, Scaponia is a great little getaway for the day, or night.

Gather your marshmallows, chocolate, and graham crackers and settle round the campfire to make s'mores. And while you're at it listen, you may hear the footsteps of a ghostly man and his dog. On a full moon night, you might even catch a brief glimpse of them. The man is the ghost of a horse thief who got caught sitting in front of a fire in his own cabin. Beside him sat his dog, growling fiercely as a vigilante mob rushed the cabin.

Stealing another's horse may not have been a capital offense in the early days of the West as far as lawmen were concerned, but vigilantes, those who took law into their own hands, saw it differently. Stealing a horse was serious business that deserved serious punishment.

The horse thief was hanged from the nearest tall tree and his dog was shot. After burying the man and his dog near his cabin, the vigilantes saddled up and moved on. That might have been the last of his horse-thieving days but not the last of the man. According to legend, the ghostly horse thief and his loyal companion wander aimlessly along the water's edge in Scaponia Park night after night. Although an encounter with the pair may be unsettling, neither the ghostly man nor his dog mean any harm.

This story made me curious, so I started researching. I know ghosts exist. I've seen them. So a ghost and his dog walking a lonely path in Scaponia Park seemed reasonable to me. But who was this man? Was he really an unfortunate horse thief? Was a horse thief hanged in Scappoose in the 1800s? I could find nothing. Of course, vigilantes probably didn't run to the nearest newspaper office boasting of their deeds. But surely someone had to know something. Finally, I found something about a horse thief in Scappoose. The story was from February 26, 1909, in the *Oregonian*. It seems a horse thief broke into a Portland farm and made off with a couple of prized horses. The farm's owner offered a large reward for the return of the horses. The thief headed to Scappoose with Sheriff Stevens and Deputy Bulger hot on his trail.

They found the horses in Scappoose and returned them to their rightful owner. But what happened to the horse thief? There was no mention of who he was or where he might have gone. No arrest was ever made. The thief had escaped the long arm of the law. In this case, legend doesn't follow the facts. And that brings us to the question—who is the ghostly man and dog at Scaponia Park?

Sharon Gill and Dave Oester of Seaside

I can't imagine a book about Oregon's ghosts without including the late Dave and Sharon Gill Oester. Founders of the International Ghost Hunting Society, the Seaside husband and wife team were pioneers in developing ghost-hunting classes, the electronic aspect of ghost hunting, and the originators of the orb theory (i.e., the belief that orbs in photos were ghosts). In their 1995 book, *Twilight Visitors: Ghost Tales, Volume One*, Gill and Oester recounted many stories of Oregon ghosts including some that occurred in their Seaside home.

The house was, according to the Oesters, located on 12th Avenue and was haunted with ghosts inhabiting several different areas, including the basement. During the two years they lived in the house they experienced much ghostly activity and strange noises, all coming from the basement. At one point a disembodied voice spoke to Dave in the basement. The Oesters would continue to experience ghost activity until they moved out and left the state. They eventually relocated to Arizona to continue their exploration of the paranormal. And the hauntings in Seaside continue.

Don't Play "Dancing Queen" for Me

*T*he Bridge Tender at 611 Broadway Street in Seaside is a long-time neighborhood bar housed in a building with ghosts and a past. According to legend, the upstairs area of the building was once a brothel. There are no historical records to back this up, still one of the Bridge Tender's ghosts is a beautiful lady in a green velvet dress, believed to be a former madame with a friendly disposition—as long as things go her way.

When something displeases her, the Madame, as she is known, throws a temper tantrum. She will knock on walls or move things from one place to the other. While discussing Oregon's ghosts, Rocky Smith, Director of the Oregon Ghost Conference and owner of Haunted Oregon City, shared a humorous story about Madame's musical tastes. Apparently, nothing displeased Madame more than ABBA, particularly the group's 1976 hit song "Dancing Queen."

The song was a number-one hit worldwide and inducted into the Grammy Hall of Fame in 2015. Yes, it was popular—but not with Madame. Whenever "Dancing Queen" started to play, glasses would fall over, drinks would spill, and a horrible racket could be heard along with ABBA. At first it was funny. But it eventually got so bad that the song had to be removed from the jukebox. Madame was happy and peace was restored.

There are a couple of children haunting the Bridge Tender as well. A boy and a girl about seven or eight; however, the kids aren't content to stay in one building. They move from one nearby shop to the next. The kids aren't seen often, but people have heard them noisily running around and the children's song "Pop Goes the Weasel."

Bandage Man Seaside

*A*t the junction between Highways 26 and 101, there is the story of a ghost who seems eerily similar to Cannon Beach's Bandage Man. The Seaside ghost jumps into the back of pick-up trucks and frightens drivers by pounding on the windows and the cab. He is angry. Ask yourself why. Then stop the truck and try to find out what is going on. This is when he will vanish, leaving behind a pile of bloody bandages. Because Seaside is only around eight and a half miles from Cannon Beach, it's possible that Bandage Man spends his time between the two cities.

St. Helens: Halloween's a Very Big Deal

*D*uring their 1805 exploration of the northwest the Lewis and Clark expedition passed through what is present-day St. Helens. More than 200 years later, explorers to this small city come for Halloween. If Halloween happens to be your favorite holiday, you should know about this historic town on the Columbia River.

Only 30 miles northwest of Portland, St. Helens is a town that embraces Halloween with a fun family event, the Spirit of Halloween Town. And it's a long celebration lasting from mid-September until the last night of October. A filming location for the 1998 Disney film, *Halloweentown*, St. Helens thought about it, and then, like a materializing apparition, the spooky festival at the Riverside District began to take shape. There are witches, scarecrows, and goblins, pumpkins and costumes, and of course, ghosts. And that's where we come in.

Let's stop at the St. Helens City Hall (the old courthouse) and the Columbia County Courthouse behind these buildings is approximately the location where 27-year-old August Schieve made history by being the first and only person to be hanged in St. Helens (Columbia County). Schieve was convicted for murdering Joseph Shulkowski the day after Christmas 1901. During the trial Schieve's father took responsibility for the murder. Jurors thought he was trying to save his son from the gallows and ignored him.

August Schieve proclaimed his innocence all the way to his execution. No one believed him. On July 2, 1902, his sentence was carried out. On his deathbed, Schieve's father spoke of the murder of Shulkowski, claiming it was him and not his son, who had waylaid and killed Shulkowski for the money he had on his person.

We will never know who killed Shulkowski. But we do know that August Schieve may not rest in peace in his lonely grave in Trenholm. Legend has it that his father John shares the grave with him.

Which of them was guilty? Perhaps we should ask the ghostly man who appears at this spot on certain nights when the mist sweeps in off the water. Surely the ghost is either that of August or John Schieve.

A stop at the old Klondike Hotel is surely in order for those on a ghost quest. Built to accommodate the men who worked in the shipyards and local loggers in 1906, the Klondike served as a hotel, bar, and brothel. Much of the old building was demolished 50 years later; the upstairs area was closed off, and the remaining portion of the building was then used as a restaurant. It is in the darkened hallway upstairs that ghost activity usually occurs, although disembodied voices have been heard throughout the building. Sightings include a transparent woman in white who may have been murdered in the brothel upstairs and an elegantly dressed man complete with top hat. If you were a fan of the TV shows *Ghost Hunters* and *Paranormal State*, you've probably seen the Klondike Hotel.

Over at the historic Columbia Theater, noisy ghost kids run up and down the aisles, and up in the balcony, a ghostly old man rocks the seats back and forth. Either he is laughing or crying, but one thing's for sure—all that rocking is a good way to jostle a box of popcorn and spill a soft drink.

The ghosts are here in St. Helens all year round, but it's at Halloween when they really come into their own.

A Milwaukie Ghost Story

Things are seldom what they seem.

—W. S. Gilbert

Not to be confused with that city in Wisconsin that spells its name differently, Milwaukie is located in the northern most part of Oregon. Dessert lovers will be happy to know that Milwaukie is home to the Bing cherry. And that makes it special to me. Can't you just see all those lattice top pies and cherries jubilee flambé? I can. I can also see what Gilbert meant about things not always being what they seem in this story.

The sun was barely up on Sunday morning, January 2, 1910, when gardener Matto Ignato began his walk along the bicycle path at the Milwaukie Cemetery. A cold morning, Ignato shivered as he walked. Suddenly in the distance something caught his eye—a ghost, crawling up from out of a grave. Ignato turned and started running and screaming in terror. He wanted no part of ghosts this morning, or ever for that matter.

He jumped the cemetery fence and grabbed the first passerby he saw.

"Ghost! There's a ghost in the cemetery!" he yelled, pointing toward the spot where he'd seen the ghost.

Curious, the passerby headed toward the direction Ignato had pointed. And on closer inspection he discovered that the ghost was actually Thomas Neal, gravedigger, preparing a grave for a funeral. Apparently Ignato had seen him climbing out of the grave with a boulder and assumed he was a ghost.

Ignato had already gone home, thinking he'd encountered a real live ghost. No one bothered telling him any different.

Southern Oregon

My Chef Is a Ghost

Cooking may be as much a means of self-expression as any of the arts.

—Fannie Farmer

In Hell they are probably serving biscuits that didn't rise, gravy that never thickened, and steaks so tough they would break the spirit and the blade of any knife. Much like writing, cooking is both an art and a craft. It all depends on who's in the kitchen. The following story is for anyone whose mother-in-law, friend, or spouse ever criticized their cooking ability.

In *The World (Coos Bay Oregon) Newspaper* on February 14, 1989, there was a story about a Bandon woman who couldn't cook. That's easily remedied and what the internet is for—except in 1989 there was no internet. If one wanted to learn to cook, one had to take cooking classes or consult a few cookbooks. Of course, there were always frozen dinners and can openers. Many resorted to a third option—trial and error. A lot of failed meals went down the garbage disposal as a result of the trial-and-error method.

The woman in our story chose yet another approach; she consulted a ghost. *Sacre bleu!* Not just any ghost but a ghostly French chef by the name of Jacques. *Mais oui!* Jacques was willing to impart some cooking knowledge and recipes. He shared enough cooking secrets so that this woman was able to create a cookbook (which I have desperately sought online and off to no avail.) It would be most interesting to see what recipes and tips Jacques shared. *Mon dieu,* stir the *béchamel* and watch that soufflé!

If you're so inclined to search for it, the title of the book is *Ghost Cooking*, and the author is Georgia Lubeck. Maybe you will have better luck in locating the book than I did.

The Witch at Lafayette Pioneer Cemetery

This quiet Dust was Gentlemen and Ladies;
And Lads and Girls
Was laughter and sighing
And frocks and curls.

—Emily Dickinson

*O*f course, there are ghosts in Lafayette Pioneer Cemetery. But the one that is most often encountered here is not a resident. She is buried 254 miles north in the Jacksonville Cemetery in Jacksonville. A mother's undying love is the reason she chooses to haunt the Lafayette Pioneer Cemetery.

Her story is known locally as the Lafayette Gypsy Curse. And it begins when Richard Marple was hanged in Lafayette on November 11, 1887. Marple had been convicted of hacking shopkeeper David Corker to death with an axe and then dismembering the body. His alleged accomplice in the brutal murder was his mother, Anna. Because there wasn't enough evidence to convict her, Anna was not tried.

And so she stood nearby on a gray November day behind a tall fence that had been erected for the event. The fence prevented the 300 onlookers from seeing the actual hanging. But they could hear. As Anna's beloved son was being escorted to the gallows, the sheriff ordered that a black hood be placed over his head. The noose was slipped around his neck, and he was hanged. His was not a swift death. Somehow the noose knot caught under his chin and his neck wasn't broken. It would take 18 agonizing minutes for Marple to die.

Hysterical and sobbing loudly, Anna cursed Lafayette and all its citizens to fire. "Lafayette will never prosper," she screamed. "It will be destroyed by three fires. Mark my word!"

Richard Marple's life slowly slipped away. His body was taken down, buried in Lafayette Pioneer Cemetery, and forgotten. But Anna's words were not. There were those who lived in fear believing Anna Marple to be a witch. Whether she was a witch or not, fire has raged through the town twice since Anna's curse. When her daughter-in-law packed up and left Lafayette, Anna moved to Jacksonville and lived out her life.

In death she came back to Lafayette. At least she is at the cemetery. Those who've seen the misty gray figure of the old woman say she still weeps for her long-lost son, Richard. Shortly after Richard Marple's execution, a cellmate came forward claiming that Marple had confessed his part and that of his mother, in the murder of David Corker. What's more, the cellmate said that Marple boasted of two other axe murders. If this is true, Anna Marple was as evil as her son.

Local lore holds that she was indeed an evil witch. And she is so miserable and unhappy that she delights in terrifying anyone who happens to cross her path. Stay out of her way.

Anna Marple is not the only ghost at the Lafayette Pioneer Cemetery. The tragic Lena Elsie Imus of the Argyle Winery is also buried there. Although her favorite haunt is the winery, Lena makes an occasional appearance at the cemetery. The very idea of encountering a ghost in an old cemetery on a moonless night may be unsettling to many people, but unlike Anna, Lena is kindly and doesn't want to frighten anyone. Most likely it is Lena's laughter that people have reportedly heard in the cemetery because Anna has nothing to laugh about.

Ghosts of Crater Lake

*L*ocated in the Cascade Range, Oregon's only national Park, Crater Lake, was formed more then 7,000 years ago with the eruption and collapse of volcano, Mt. Mazama. The deepest lake in the US and the seventh deepest in the world, Crater Lake is also known to be one of the world's clearest lakes. The Klamath American Indian tribes that have lived in this region for more than 10,000 years called the lake *giiwas* and considered it a sacred place—too sacred even for human eyes.

According to Klamath legend, the lake was created as a result of a battle between two spirits, and to so much as gaze on its crystal-clear waters will bring death, destruction, and sorrow. But how can you not gaze at it? The lake is stunning with water so blue it seems almost unreal. Of the many legends concerning Crater Lake, the most unsettling is that of the vicious water devils who once guarded the lake. Getting down to the water was no easy feat. Anyone who dared to do so was in danger, especially if they got too close to the water's edge. This infuriated the water devils who then pulled the encroachers down into the lake's watery depths—and certain death.

Sightings of Bigfoot (Sasquatch) also abound here at Crater Lake. Then too, there are the ghosts. This shouldn't surprise anyone because ghost researchers will tell you, violent or unexpected death often leads to a haunting.

And many strange disappearances, violent and unexpected deaths have occurred at Crater Lake. In November 1933, two young women, Doris Sparks and Andrea Mardelle, set out from Spokane to meet up with Doris's fiancé in Klamath Falls 517 miles south. They never made it. While driving through the Crater Lake National Park Doris Sparks and Andrea Mardelle disappeared. Their bodies were discovered five months later beneath the wreckage of their car. They'd driven around a road closed sign and tried to turn around.

The car crashed through a guard rail, tumbling down 150 feet and lay hidden under heavy snow.

For all the accidental, strange, and suicidal deaths that have occurred here, murder has also happened. On July 21, 1952, the bodies of Charles Patrick Culhane and Albert Marston Jones, two visiting General Motors executives, were discovered in a secluded wooded area. Fully clothed and shoeless, the men had been gagged, and their hands tied behind their backs. They'd been shot execution-style, in the back of the head at close range—only a mile or so from where their green 1951 Pontiac was discovered on Highway 62, near Annie Creek Canyon. The car's front doors were open, and the keys were still in the ignition. The murders have never been solved.

In August 1970, a new park ranger got lost while looking for the 1945 site of a F6F Hellcat fighter plane crash that claimed its young pilot's life. As he sat on a log trying to get his bearings, the park ranger stopped and looked around, all the while feeling as if someone was staring at him. Imagine his surprise when he looked toward a log and saw a skull looking back at him. He was a half-mile from the crash site near Mt. Scott. Later the US Navy would identify the skull as that of the young pilot who'd died there 25 years before.

More than half a million people visit Crater Lake every year. Some of them encounter the paranormal in the form of ghostly sightings and unexplained noises. On Wizard Island, a campfire with several people standing around it has been reported to rangers several times. When rangers arrive, there is no campfire, no evidence of a campfire, and no living people other than themselves.

Oregon Caves Chateau

I know I am but summer to your heart.

—Edna St. Vincent Millay

*T*he antithesis to happily-ever-after wedded bliss is the story of the young bride whose husband abandoned her on their wedding night. Although there are many variations to this tale, the bride's name remains the same in all of them—Elizabeth. And she is known to haunt room 310 of the Oregon Caves Chateau. She is not a hateful or spiteful ghost, but there is a negative aura about her. This is understandably so. Just how the ghostly Elizabeth came to haunt room 310 depends on which variation of her story you believe.

The Oregon Caves deep within Siskiyou Mountains was discovered in 1874, and the Oregon Caves National Monument was established in 1909 by President Taft. By the time Elizabeth and her groom came here sometime in the 1930s, thousands of people had visited the caves, making it a popular tourist destination.

Anxious to freshen up for dinner, Elizabeth, went into the bathroom and gazed into the mirror. As she thought of the future she and her groom would share, Elizabeth smiled broadly. Like all brides before her, and since, she assured herself that no one had ever been happier than she was at this moment. Satisfied that she looked radiant, she called to her husband for help with the clasp of her necklace. Silence returned her call, so she called to him again. Why wasn't he responding? What had happened? She stepped out into the room to find it empty. Where had he gone? He probably stepped out for a bit of fresh air. She waited and waited. When he didn't return Elizabeth set off down the hall to find him.

At the far end of the hallway, she passed an open door and suddenly stopped at the sound of a woman's laughter, followed by her husband's voice. She stepped inside the room. Her husband had his arms wrapped around another woman.

"You should have stayed in the room," he said angrily.

"What?" Elizabeth cried.

Her dreams dashed and her world destroyed, Elizabeth stumbled back to her room, opened the window, and leapt to her death.

Another version of this story has Elizabeth hanging herself in the room. Yet another story has her husband angrily shoving her out the window. Regardless of how she died, Elizabeth left this world a brokenhearted woman. But she hasn't gone very far. She is sometimes heard sobbing loudly in one of the hall closets. She will sometimes move items from one place to another. The ghostly Elizabeth is occasionally seen walking the third-floor hall and weeping. Those who've stayed in any of the rooms on the third floor report hearing strange noises and feelings of apprehension.

It's rumored that the chateau won't even book guests into room 310 unless all the other rooms are full. And that's probably as much for Elizabeth's benefit as it is the guests. Some have suggested that Elizabeth is waiting for her errant husband, hoping that he will have a change of heart and return to her in the afterlife. That's doubtful after all these years, but anything's possible, even the transformation of a cheating husband.

Charles Laughton's Last Curtain Call

When we are born, we cry that we are come to this
great stage of fools.

—*King Lear*, William Shakespeare

*C*harles Laughton died in 1962 at the age of 63; as successful as he was, the actor had one wish that went unfulfilled. And this leads us to our next story that's been told and retold countless times.

A classically trained actor who learned his craft at London's Royal Academy of Dramatic Art, Laughton starred in numerous productions at London's Old Vic Theater. And Broadway beckoned with more roles—and better roles. The actor and his wife, actress Elsa Lancaster, left Great Britain for the US where he would star in several Broadway productions; in 1932 he appeared in his first Hollywood film, *The Old Dark House.*

Film was not new to him, but he was new to Hollywood and the film industry was impressed. Soon he was being sought for other roles. It didn't take Laughton long to realize that Hollywood was the land of opportunity for him; he and his wife packed up and moved to southern California. Once there, they became US citizens.

A wise decision because Charles Laughton would never want for a role. In 1933 he won an Academy Award for best actor for his role as Henry VIII in the film *The Private Life of Henry VIII.* He would be nominated for an Academy Award two more times in his career. However, he would not win again.

Although film was where he would achieve his greatest success, Laughton never lost his love for the theater. By the time he reached his 60s, Laughton was wealthy and famous for having played many interesting characters onscreen. In 1961 after attending the Shakespeare Festival in Ashland, he realized there were two roles he desperately wanted to play at the Elizabethan Theater: *King Lear* and Falstaff in the *Merry Wives of Windsor*.

In his book *As I Remember, Adam: A Biography of a Festival*, Angus Bowmer wrote that he and Laughton had discussions and the actor was scheduled to play the parts in 1963 after his latest film *Irma La Douce* was completed.

However, Laughton would not live to play King Lear or Falstaff. He died of cancer on December 15, 1962. Apparently, the disappointment was so great for the actor that he determined not even death would keep him from the theater and the role he coveted. Whenever *King Lear* is performed at the Elizabethan Theater, the ghostly Laughton is said to make an appearance somewhere there.

Of course, he is always in full costume. No doubt Laughton plays the role of ghost to perfection. After all, he played Sir Simon de Canterville (the ghost) in the 1944 classic *The Canterville Ghost*. There are times when the ghostly actor chooses not to be seen, but he can still be heard sighing loudly or laughing uproariously.

The Blue Lady of Lithia Park

*A*t 93 acres, Lithia Park is the largest park in Ashland. The land-scaper for the park was John McLaren, who was the superin-tendent for San Francisco's Golden Gate Park. There is yet another connection to Golden Gate Park—a ghostly connection.

She is the blue lady; believed to be the victim of a long-ago sexual assault and murder, the shimmering blue ghost appears at the duck pond. The blue lady doesn't give anyone time to gaze. She appears quickly and vanishes just as quickly. If you're listening closely, you may hear the faint sound of weeping as well.

Ghosts at the University

*S*outhern Oregon University in Ashland has been called one of the most haunted campuses in the US. Founded in 1872, the university has gone through numerous name changes in its more than a century of existence. In 1997 it was renamed Southern Oregon University (SOU). Perhaps this name will be as permanent as the ghosts who see the university as their forever home.

Let's stop first at Suzanne Holmes Residence Hall where students sometimes encounter a little boy who is soaking wet and begging for a towel. Before anyone can figure out how to help him, the child vanishes into thin air. According to legend, the little boy drowned in the basement of the building as it was being built in the 1930s.

The Plunkett Center has an interesting history and is considered by many to be the site of most paranormal activity on the SOU campus. Originally called the Chappell/Swedenburg House, it was built in 1904 for Charles Chappell. When Chappell died suddenly in 1905, Dr. Francis G. Swedenburg purchased the house. And in 1906, he and his new bride Olive moved in. The house would remain in the Swedenburg family for the next 59 years. In 1965 the Chappell/Swedenburg House became part of the SOU campus. Today the Plunkett Center is used for different events and houses the SOU alumni office on the first floor.

Cold breezes, jiggling door handles, stomping sounds, and the feeling of being watched have also been reported at Plunkett Center. One of the most frightening stories involves a séance that took place sometime in the early 1960s. Using a Ouija board for their séance, participants called for any spirits present to come forward and communicate. Imagine their surprise when the Ouija board was snatched from the table by unseen hands and tossed out the window. Clearly, the séance didn't turn out as expected. The participants may have received more communication than they wanted.

They ran down the stairs and out the door. Had they created a pathway for something dark and malicious—or were they just the actions of a playful ghost?

Although no one can say with certainty, it seems more than coincidence that this is where most of the university's paranormal activity is centered.

The Ghosts of Golden

*H*ere's something you can use if you're ever asked about it on the game show *Jeopardy*. Oregon has more ghost towns than any other state in the US. Of the state's more than 200 ghost towns, Golden is listed on the *National Register of Historic Places* and is owned by Oregon Parks and Recreation Department. Episodes of the series *Bonanza* were filmed here in the 1960s, as were some movies. For this reason, some may question whether the buildings here are props or original to the early town. Authenticity doesn't seem to bother Golden's ghosts who've taken up residence throughout the tiny town.

There are four structures in Golden that was known as the "Driest Town in Oregon." No, that wasn't because of a drought. The town's founder William Ruble was a religious teetotaler who didn't want anyone drinking, dancing, and hanging out in saloons in his town. Thus, there were two churches and no saloons. Not to worry about those who weren't allowed an ice-cold beer after a long day toiling for gold at nearby Coyote Creek. They traveled to the next town where saloons were abundant, and alcohol flowed freely.

Golden was not a big town. And yet when you look at the few buildings that remain in the picturesque ghost town it's difficult to imagine that Golden was once the home of more than 150 people. Most were miners who'd come here seeking gold. By 1920 the gold was gone, the post office was closed, and the town was abandoned—until the ghosts discovered Golden.

These ghosts could be those of William Ruble and some of his most ardent followers. And they've returned here to Golden to see that no one is drinking or dancing. Ruble was an ordained minister who considered himself and his followers pious. And yet rumor is that the ghostly residents of Golden are strictly a negative bunch.

A honeymooning couple that visited Golden on a warm summer day shared a strange story. They wandered through the little town and then, as newlyweds do, they stopped for a quick kiss and a couple of selfies. And this seemed to have attracted the attention of a menacing figure in a black cloak who was suddenly staring at them from several yards off. Odd to wrap up in such a heavy cloak on a summer day, they thought. They couldn't tell if it was a man or a women. From then on, it followed them. Wherever they went, there it was—always at a distance.

"Why are you following us?" demanded the young husband. "Leave us alone."

Intent on getting a photo, the wife pointed her phone at the figure. As she did so an unearthly growl emanated from the figure as it turned from them and vanished into the warm summer air. They'd encountered a ghost and suddenly they were very cold.

You may say this is nothing but a trick of light, *folie à deux*, or overworked imaginations. But how can you be sure?

Bigfoot versus the Ghost

Several years ago, my family decided to get away from the city for a week; we set out for an Oregon vacation in the woods. In a time long before the internet, we found the perfect place in a magazine ad—a rustic two-bedroom kitchenette cabin, far from the madding crowd. To city dwellers tired of snarled freeways and crowded spaces, knotty pine walls and a nearby babbling brook seemed like heaven. A picturesque little place called the Humbug Lodge near the Rogue River was our destination.

As the car made its way along twisted roads, large signs informed us that we were in Bigfoot Country. Bigfoot as in Sasquatch and that was all fine and good, but given the choice, we preferred ghosts. Surely there was some weeping lady or headless lumberjack with a nice backstory wandering the woods after dark. These would be much easier to deal with than an elusive Bigfoot. Still we were going to the woods where there was no TV; we would cook simple one-pan meals and sit by a fireplace, listening to that babbling brook promised in the magazine ad.

We'd forgotten that spiders and bugs inhabit the woods and that one-pan meals tend to stick when using an old cast iron pan instead of easy-peasy nonstick. We were roughing it. After the kitchen was cleaned, and showers taken, we settled in for a game of Monopoly and the sounds of nature. The silence was broken by a horrible screeching noise that arose in the darkness.

"That's an owl!" my husband assured us.

Next came a roar that sounded vaguely like that of a lion. "A bobcat!" my husband said calmly.

I'd seen enough Wild Kingdom to know that wasn't a bobcat.

"Whatever that is, it's no bobcat," I said.

"It's Bigfoot!" the kids screamed making for the window. There was nothing but darkness. They headed for the front door, but I stopped them in their tracks.

"Don't you dare open that door!" I warned.

A ghost I could deal with. But I wanted no part of whatever creatures were making those noises. And so it went. We heard one strange noise after another until bedtime.

"Bigfoot and the ghost are fighting," the kids laughed.

It did sound like that. But as long as they kept it out of our cabin I didn't care.

Long after the kids had fallen asleep, we pulled the curtains back and peered out the window. Even in the full moon night stars were shining brighter than they ever did in our light polluted city.

"Look!" my husband whispered.

There was movement. Something was running off in the distance.

"Bigfoot?" I asked.

"Not unless he glows."

"A ghost?" I asked happily. Things were now getting interesting.

Before he could answer, something leaped onto the glowing figure that held a threatening stance. "They are fighting," I said.

"It looks like they're wrestling."

Suddenly the ghostly figure ran up to the window. Snarling and screeching and roaring, the sounds of the woods were all around us.

"This is the best part! Please tell me I'm not dreaming," I cried to my husband, pulling the covers over my head.

He didn't say a word. He was fast asleep beside me in the bed.

Rock Point Cemetery

Be silent in that solitude, Which is not loneliness—
for then.
The spirits of the dead, who stood. In life before
thee, are again. In death around thee, and their will.

—Edgar Allan Poe

*R*ock Point Cemetery is at least a hundred years old. It's located little more than a mile from Gold Hill and the mysterious Oregon Vortex with its House of Mystery, which was originally built in 1904 to serve as the assay office for the Old Grey Eagle Mining Company. And this, they say, is the problem. Although there are those that might insist the Oregon Vortex and House of Mystery is nothing more than optical illusion, others say there is something else at work here and that's what to blame for the strange paranormal activity and ghost that haunt the old Rock Point Cemetery.

A thousand people are buried at Rock Point Cemetery; some of them rest in unmarked graves. And that fact alone can give rise to ghostly activity. Who wants to rest unacknowledged?

The resident specter of Rock Point Cemetery has piercing red eyes that glow like embers, wears a long, black, hooded robe, and carries a lantern. He silently walks past the headstones as if he is looking for someone. If you should encounter him don't say a word or call out because if he realizes that he's been spotted, he will disappear. Come to think of it, that might not be a bad idea.

Another strange occurrence here at Rock Point Cemetery is the green mist that seems to cover certain graves on moonless nights. The mist slowly moves along from one grave to the next. Occasionally stopping to hover over random graves, the unearthly green mist then vanishes as quickly as it appeared.

There aren't many ghosts walking around cemeteries during the daylight hours, but a ghostly elderly man wanders here among the headstones, talking softly to himself. If you should stop and wish him good morning or good afternoon, he will vanish without a word right before your eyes.

A ghost is a ghost day or night and some are perturbed by their first encounter. This might be a good time to buckle up and leave Rock Point Cemetery. But those who are driving should know about the cemetery's cracked windshield legend. It seems that the windshields of cars passing by the Rock Point Cemetery have been known to crack for no apparent reason. And yes, the Oregon Vortex is also blamed for this bit of weirdness.

Linkville Playhouse

Remember: there are no small parts, only small actors.

—Constantin Stanislavski

No actor wants to leave the stage. This is just another reason why theaters are haunted. Think of it. There's the thrill of opening night, curtain call, and the audience applause of approval. It's heady stuff; once it's in your blood, there is no exit stage left. You can't walk away, even after death has claimed you.

And this brings us to the ghost at the Linkville Playhouse in Klamath Falls. There's no secret as to his identity. Some of those involved with the theater know that he's a former actor who died in 1992. And yet, he has been seen numerous times since then, sitting in the audience in row 22 or 23 and smoking a pipe. You may see him during dress rehearsals, but he doesn't stay long and appears and disappears quickly.

The ghostly actor isn't performing a one-man show. There is another ghost on the premises. And he is more playful. He moves things around, will turn lights on and off, and may even be responsible for the weird music that occasionally emanates from the theater's attic.

Maud Baldwin and the Ghosts of the Baldwin Hotel Museum

> I am going insane and cannot stand it. You will find me in the lake.
>
> —Maud Baldwin's suicide note

As the only daughter of Oregon businessman and senator George Baldwin and his wife Josephine, Maud Baldwin's future might have seemed assured. It wasn't. Instead, two family tragedies would send Maud's life spiraling in a downward trajectory.

At a time when women weren't being encouraged to go to college, she studied photography at the California College of Photography in Palo Alto. She excelled at her craft and is noted today for her photography, which consists of thousands of photographs of early day Klamath Falls.

Sadly, Maud never got the chance to live the life she'd dreamed of. This may be why she haunts the Baldwin Hotel Museum.

The Baldwin Hotel was built in 1905 at 31 Main Street in Klamath Falls. Originally used as a hardware store, the building was converted to the Baldwin Hotel in 1911. Much of the four-story, 40-room building looks the same as it did when George and Josephine Baldwin owned it. The hotel was closed 60 years later in 1971.

When George Baldwin died in 1920, he believed his daughter Maud was the best person to oversee the hotel, so he left the hotel in her care. He may have thought otherwise, but Baldwin hadn't done his daughter any favors. Maud had also taken on the task of caring for her invalid mother, who'd recently suffered a stroke. With no help from her siblings, Maud was soon overwhelmed. Between her mother's care and the added responsibility of the hotel, there was no time for her one true love—photography.

Three years later, to ease some of her burden, Maud sold the Baldwin Hotel. That same year romance unexpectedly came into her life. Prince Charming came to her in the form of a restaurant cook. And suddenly, Maud was in love. The world was no longer such a grim and unhappy place. Sadly, the object of Maud's affection wasn't in love with her. He didn't want to stay in one place too long. When he packed up his wire whisk and other cooking accouterments and headed for Alaska a year later, he went alone. He hadn't even asked Maud to join him, and she was devastated.

Heartbroken and still recovering from the loss of her beloved father, Maud hung on as long as she could. And then on May 22, 1926, she decided. She wrote her note and crossed the street to the section of the river known as Lake Ewauna and walked in. She is buried at Linkville Pioneer Cemetery near her father and mother.

There are those who believe that she has returned to the Baldwin Hotel Museum. Much of the museum is as it was in her lifetime, and her photography studio remains untouched. And this is the ideal trigger object, which is, according to ghost investigators, something that will be special or have personal meaning to a ghost. So this is where you'll usually find the ghostly Maud Baldwin who announces herself with an icy breeze. Be prepared; she may appear anytime day or night. The ghostly Maud seems content as she wanders through her studio.

Also in residence are former tenants of the hotel who've been seen standing at the windows in the early morning hours before the sun has risen. A ghostly old man who lived at the hotel for more than 50 years is believed to walk the halls much as he did in life. He is blamed for unexplained noises. There is nothing like the familiar (a trigger object) to draw a ghost, I suppose.

Eastern Oregon

Malheur Butte

*M*alheur Butte is a strange looking hill. It's not a hill at all but an extinct volcano that stands 2,661 feet tall and dates back millions of years. No wonder the ghosts that are associated with this place are not your average garden-variety ones. In French, *malheur* literally means "bad hour." Misfortune and bad luck are exactly what they say some have experienced here at Malheur Butte.

Before we get started in our exploration, please be aware that much of the land around Malheur Butte is private property. And one thing no self-respecting ghost hunter ever wants to do is trespass.

According to legend, the ghosts inhabiting Malheur Butte are strange grotesque creatures with a negative aura about them. Ghostly people in robes involved in some sort of ritual have been seen here numerous times as well. Local lore holds that these are the ghosts of evil witches who held their coven meetings at Malheur Butte long ago.

Now I'll tell you that as a ghost research/historian, I don't believe that. I think someone gave their imagination free reign regarding these ghosts. Although I don't doubt that ghosts are here at Malheur Butte, I believe these phantoms to be something entirely different.

Some ghost stories are just that—stories. Others have a ring of authenticity, with details that can be verified historically. In trying to determine one from the other and find the causation of paranormal activity it is prudent to examine a location's history. In looking at Oregon's history we find documented evil activity of people in robes and hoods that dates to a century ago, and they were certainly not witches.

During the early 1920s, the scurrilous Ku Klux Klan brought their racist hatred to Oregon. By looking at the old photographs of groups of hooded Ku Klux Klan members we can easily see a correlation between them and the enrobed ghosts that have been reportedly seen here for decades. With this in mind, I believe that the evil ghostly people in robes holding meetings here at Malheur Butte are actually the ghosts of long-dead Ku Klux Klan members. And the ghost witch stories were told as a cover for the secret meetings being held here.

Evil leaves scorched earth as far as hauntings go; these ghostly people may be imprinted here and may stay here for millions of years, much like Malheur Butte itself, reliving their hate-filled rituals into eternity.

That Time Elvis's Ghost Came to the Museum

*O*nce upon a time in the music industry, Elvis Presley was the "king of rock and roll." That time was from the mid-1950s until one night in August 1977 when the king died a solitary death.

The music world mourned its king, and the rest of the world moved on. In 1982, Graceland was opened to the public so that fans who wanted a glimpse of how the king had lived—and died— could satisfy their curiosity. Paying homage, they toured his mid-20th-century opulent mansion, gawked at some of his garish attire, stepped onto his private jet, and finally stopped at his grave. Along the way some of these visitors claimed to have caught a glimpse of the ghostly Elvis, walking among them. And it may have been. Apparently, Elvis as a ghost was getting around more than Elvis on tour.

Although we all know that Vegas tops the list of ghostly Elvis sightings—not counting impersonators of course—the city of Redmond, Oregon, can also lay claim to having been visited by afterlife Elvis. He arrived on his tour bus Taking Care of Business (TCB). Not a fan of flying, Elvis toured the US in his custom 1976 Motor Coach Industries (MCI) Crusader two or three times.

According to Sharon Gill and Dave Oester in their 1995 book, *Twilight Visitors: Ghost Tales, Volume One*, some believed the spirit of Elvis was on that bus when it arrived at the Fantastic Museum in Redmond. While exploring the bus, Gill and Oester got some high electromagnetic field readings and several fans that had come aboard the bus were getting all shook up because they could sense the presence of Elvis. Although no one saw him, they knew that Elvis was near.

Nothing lasts forever. The Fantastic Museum closed. The bus was sold to a company in Texas, and Elvis went back to haunting Graceland and Las Vegas.

Elgin Opera House

Known as the Jewel of the Blue Mountains, the tiny town of Elgin is proud of its Opera House. Completed in 1912, the Elgin Opera House was created with a dual purpose in mind. In a cost-effective move, city leaders decided to use the two-story brick building to house city government offices and also as an entertainment venue.

The ghost story connected to Elgin may well be true, but as we'll soon see, it isn't historically accurate. According to the tale, sometime in the 1880s, two cowhands were competing for the hand of the same young lady. As the competition heated up the would-be suitors grew angry and fierce. One challenged the other to a gunfight in which the winner would marry the young lady, and the loser, well, he'd take up permanent residence in the town's cemetery.

On the agreed upon night, the two men met on the steps of the opera house to shoot it out. Unfortunately, both died in the ensuing gun battle. Late at night their ghosts are sometimes seen on the opera house stairs still engaged in the gun battle. The problem is that the Elgin Opera House wasn't built until 1912; the men would have had to meet elsewhere for their deadly duel. And why is there nothing in this tale that sheds some light on what the young lady thought of the arrangement?

Surely, she had some thoughts on the duel and would have had some input. Nonetheless it's a good story. And who knows, the gun-happy ghosts may be two long-dead actors, guilty of overacting and getting carried away with their roles.

Elgin High School

*E*lgin High in Elgin is a small school with not much more than a hundred students—and two ghosts. The story is of two long-ago students that were killed in a horrific car accident on their way to a school basketball game. Apparently, the teenagers really wanted to see that game. Even today, staff and students tell of hearing raucous noises that sound eerily similar to a basketball game in the empty gymnasium: a dribbling ball, a referee's whistle, cheers from a crowd, all disembodied.

It's said that when they're not watching an unearthly basketball game, the two ghosts can sometimes be spotted walking the school grounds hand in hand.

Candy Cane Park Murder

Hell is empty and all the devils are here.

—William Shakespeare

Candy Cane Park, the name might fool you into conjuring up visions of a jolly plastic Santa complete with reindeers and rows of tantalizing red-and-white candy cane decorations. But you can stop right there. Known as Hatchet Park, Candy Cane Park in central La Grande has a dark and terrifying history.

It all began on the night of February 12, 1983, when 21-year-old Dana Lynn DuMars was working as a swing shift cocktail waitress at a local tavern. She lived just a few blocks from her job, and she often walked home alone. She did so on this night, and even though it was late when she got off, Dana felt safe walking by herself in the dark. After all, La Grande was a small town and this was a safe neighborhood. The cool night air probably felt good to her, after spending hours cooped up in the smoke-filled bar. As she walked, she may have made plans for what she would do tomorrow or the next day.

Unfortunately, someone else was walking nearby that Saturday night. And he was stumbling down drunk and seething with rage at a bartender who'd treated him badly and kicked him out of the tavern for his behavior. Worse, she'd made a fool of him and embarrassed him in front of his friends. And now he wanted revenge.

DuMars hadn't said or done anything to him, but she resembled the bartender that had angered him earlier in the evening. It would be Dana's misfortune to encounter this rage-filled man who hacked her to death with an axe while trying to decapitate her. Barely alive when she was discovered the next morning, she would not live to see another day. The killer was subsequently arrested, tried, and convicted of the murder. He would serve only a few years before winning an appeal and being released.

Ever since that terrible night in 1983, Candy Cane Park has been referred to as Hatchet Park. And the ghost of the young woman who died so horrifically has been seen in certain areas of Candy Cane Park. Legend has it that the ghost liked to ride the merry-go-round where she was slaughtered. She was rumored to even shove people off the ride. For whatever reason, the merry-go-round was removed from the park 20 years after the murder.

In all likelihood, this was done as a precaution as a safety measure. It's also possible it was removed in the hopes the ghostly appearances would stop. If so, it hasn't worked. Even today nearly 40 years after her death, people report seeing the ghostly young woman as she makes her way through the park.

The Lodge at Hot Lake Springs

*A*dmittedly TV shows that feature ghosts and haunted locations have come a long way over the years. An early TV show on the Fox family channel called The Scariest Places on Earth began its run in early 2000. This was several years before Zak Bagans and the *Ghost Adventures* made ghosts, and investigating them, an acceptable endeavor—something the entire family can enjoy. The premise of scariest places was to have ordinary people and their friends visit and explore a severely haunted location for the evening.

As fate would have it, my husband Bill and I, along with a couple of our friends, appeared on the 24th episode of season 2 of *The Scariest Places on Earth*. Accompanied by a black lab named Ridley, we made our way through the haunted Goldfield Hotel. Ours was not the only haunted hot spot, there were three other locations featured on that episode and one of them happened to be Oregon's Hot Lake Hotel (Lodge).

As I watched myself on TV that October night in 2001, I had no idea that someday I would be writing about one of the other featured locations of my episode. There are no coincidences.

No one is doing much swimming here at Hot Lake Springs, one of the largest hot springs in the Pacific Northwest. With an average water temperature of 186° Fahrenheit, this water is better suited for soaking than swimming.

Long before Meriwether Lewis and William Clark's exploration that forged the Oregon Trail, which brought thousands of settlers into the region, the Nez Percé held this as their sacred place in southwestern Grande Ronde Valley. The Nez Percé called it Ea-Kesh-Pa and used the water for its restorative and therapeutic properties.

The 1811 exploration of Wilson Price Hunt that passed through this area on their journey from St. Louis, Missouri, to Astoria, opened the way for others to come. In 1836, John Jacob Astor, for whom Astoria is named, commissioned Washington Irving to write a book titled *Astoria* extolling the many virtues of the Pacific Northwest, particularly Oregon Territory and Astoria. The book was an immediate success even though Irving had never traveled to either place. The two-volume Astoria would serve the purpose of bringing even more settlers to the region.

In 1864, Samuel Newhart began work on a small resort here. When it was completed, the resort included such modern conveniences as a post office, dance hall, barbershop, drugstore, and bathhouses. The problem with the resort was its great distance from any major city; so, his resort would never become as popular as Newhart had hoped.

All this changed with the coming of the railroad 20 years later. The railroad made it easier for travelers to come to such a remote location. After Newhart's death in 1904, Dr. William Phy took over management of the resort, and it was transformed. Phy oversaw the rebuilding of the lodge. Among those who are said to have visited Hot Lake was legendary lawman and gunfighter "Wild Bill" Hickok who was shot to death on August 1, 1876, in a Deadwood saloon. Because this was nearly 30 years before Phy began overseeing the lodge, I'm guessing that if Hickok visited, it was as a ghost. And I'm sticking with this opinion until historians prove me wrong.

In 1917, after having made of it a successful venture, Phy bought the lodge and renamed it the Hot Lake Sanatorium. With the addition of a hospital facility and the waters with their curative powers, the sanatorium became so popular that people came from all over the country. Dr. William Mayo and his brother Dr. Charles Mayo, who along with their father founded the Mayo Clinic in Rochester, Minnesota, were regular visitors to the Hot Lake Sanatorium. And at one time it was known as the "Mayo Clinic of the West."

Fourteen years after purchasing the lodge, Phy died of pneumonia. Three years later a devastating fire destroyed a section of the lodge. This was during the Great Depression and business steadily declined. Over the years, the remaining section of the building was used for many different purposes. One of these was as a sanitarium. And this brings us to the screaming ghost. Believed to have been a former patient, the ghost issues forth bloodcurdling screams at all hours of the day and night.

A piano that was once located in the building was said to have belonged to the wife of Confederate leader Robert E. Lee. Although the piano is long gone, a ghostly pianist still manages to play it night after night. The music is considerably more enjoyable than the piercing screams are.

Umpqua Bank

I have no idea where the story began, but they say the building is haunted. And Umpqua Bank on East Main Street in Roseburg is one of those places we'll just have to take their word for it. Not many people are granted entry into a bank late at night, other than cleaning crews. That's understandable; ghosts don't pay attention to open and closed signs. Although ghostly people have been spotted during daylight hours in the bank, most of the action takes place after dark. Seen and not heard here in the bank is a dog that barks incessantly after dark. Perhaps there is a ghost cat about. Here kitty-kitty.

There is also a ghostly woman who is most often seen during the day. For reasons known only to herself, this ghost turns on the water faucets and flushes toilets in the women's room. She may be part of the ghostly group that scampers through the bank only to disappear into the walls. The most sinister of these bank ghosts is surely the man that waits until after midnight before turning on all the lights and staring out the window. It's anyone's guess what he is hoping to see.

Curious, over lunch one afternoon I asked a friend who once lived in Roseburg about the haunted bank. She laughed and asked, "You do know that's nonsense, right?"

"But the story's been around for a long time," I told her.

She'd lived in Roseburg. Surely she'd heard of it. She hadn't, and what's more she didn't believe a word of it. No matter what my friend thought, I know it's possible that ghosts haunt the Umpqua Bank. There is that story after all—and so I'm taking their word for it.

An Apartment in Roseburg

*A*ccording to local lore, the old Rose Apartments in Roseburg are haunted. A murder supposedly took place either on the spot where the apartment building now stands or in the building itself. Depending on the circumstances of the murder, that might be a good reason for a haunting.

Still a murder is not necessarily the reason some have encountered the paranormal at the old apartments. A shadowy apparition has appeared in certain areas of the apartment building; other indicators of ghostly activity are lights that flicker off and on and temperatures that fluctuate.

One person we will call "Edie," claimed to have been touched by a ghost several times while living in the Rose Apartments.

"It was never menacing or anything," she said. "Just more like a touch to say, 'Hey I'm here.' I got used to it after a while."

"I had just moved in and was vacuuming a new rug I'd got for the apartment the first time I was ever touched. It felt like a tap on the shoulder, and it startled me. I was by myself in my apartment at the time. Yeah, it didn't take me long to figure out it was some sort of ghost thing happening—my neighbor said she saw the ghost once, but I never did."

Applegate House: A Very Large Family of Ghosts

As part of the Great Migration of 1843, Charles and Melinda Miller Applegate and their family left Missouri and headed west. Traveling with the Applegates were Charles's brothers Lindsay and Jesse and their families.

In Oregon, the brothers settled first in Polk County before relocating to the Yoncalla Valley. Built in 1852, Charles and Melinda's house is one of the oldest known residences in the state of Oregon and was listed on the *National Register of Historic Places* in 1974. Remarkably, the house has remained in the hands of the Applegate family since it was built. The Applegate house is on private property, which means do not trespass.

According to local lore, some members of the family stay on as ghosts in their former home in Yoncalla. Charles and Melinda Applegate had 15 children. Perhaps some of them have chosen to remain at the old homestead, and they are not always quiet. When unexpected noise occurs in the upstairs area of the house, one of the Applegate kids is believed to be responsible.

The ghostly Charles and Melinda Applegate may be in residence as well. But you will not find them in the upstairs area of the house. Wanting a little peace and quiet, they are usually spotted in the parlor or the kitchen.

Ghost Soldiers of Fort Stevens State Park

*W*ith 4,300 acres of walking trails, a military museum, horseback riding, picnic tables, and a beach, Fort Stevens State Park is a state park that isn't lacking in things to see and do. Ghostly activity is but one. If you're reading this book, it's doubtful that you're bothered by the possibility of encountering a ghostly soldier, or two. And that's a good thing. Because if you should make camp here at one of largest public campgrounds in the US, chances are good you might encounter a ghost.

Originally called the Fort at Point Adams, it was built in 1863 at the height of the Civil War to prevent confederate gun boats from sailing into the mouth of the Columbia River. In 1865, the fort was completed and renamed Fort Stevens in honor of Isaac Ingall Stevens. Stevens, who served as the Territory of Washington's governor from 1853 to 1857, had attained the rank of a brigadier general in the Union Army when he was killed in action at the Battle of Chantilly in September 1862. Posthumously promoted to Major General, Stevens is buried at Newport, Rhode Island. Because he is not one of the ghostly soldiers said to walk the park during darkness, we will leave him there, resting in peace.

The first person to be buried in Fort Stevens' Post Cemetery was private August Stalberger of Company C, 2nd US Artillery. Stalberger's battered body was discovered in a creek two miles from Fort Stevens on the morning of May 19, 1868. His cause of death was originally listed as accidental due to his having fallen into the water and drowning while under the influence. But that is not the official cause of death. Stalberger, the report stated, died of blows from a person or persons unknown. The identity of the Stalberger's killer remains a mystery. So does the reason for the murder.

Perhaps this is why he wanders the grounds of the old fort. Unlike a lot of ghosts, he's not nocturnal. Stalberger is seen both day and night.

Stalberger is joined by another ghostly soldier at Fort Stevens. He is a soldier from the era of World War II who walks briskly around the fort carrying only a flashlight. Just as he did in life, the soldier keeps watch over the fort, unaware that he's been off duty for decades. Whether you choose a deluxe cabin or a tent site to camp at, the ghostly soldier is keeping watch. Over the years, campers have reported hearing his footfall as he walks through the campground in the dead of night. Others have seen him or the glowing beam of his flashlight as it cuts through early morning dense fog.

No doubt you are wondering why he is so concerned. Most likely it is because Fort Stevens was fired on during World War II by a Japanese submarine on June 21, 1942. Thus, the fort has the distinction of being the only military fort in the US to be fired on by an enemy in time of war since the War of 1812.

Sumpter and the Crescent Gold Mine

*I*f you're looking for the haunted Crescent Gold Mine, it's in Sumpter, a mining boomtown that was established in 1899. In 1917, a devastating fire destroyed 12 city blocks and almost a hundred buildings. Rather than rebuild, most residents who were affected by the fire packed up and moved on leaving Sumpter all but a ghost town.

Rumor has it that some of Sumpter's ghosts may have taken up residence in the Crescent Gold Mine and that it is so haunted no one wants to work there. Opinions are divided whether there's any validity to that. The Crescent Gold Mine was featured in the Syfy TV reality series *Ghost Mine*. While mining for gold in the abandoned mine, the show's stars may have stumbled upon a Tommy-knocker.

Western miners of the 19th and early 20th century were superstitious about the Tommy-knockers. Similar to a leprechaun, Tommy-knockers were believed to be malevolent by some. These little creatures inhabited mines and liked to play pranks on miners. They could help a man by bringing great wealth or make his job difficult, if not dangerous. It all depended on the Tommy-knocker's mood and whether a miner believed in him and was generous with his lunch. Tommy-knockers liked offerings of bread, cheese, or anything else a miner wanted to leave.

If you're eager to try your hand at finding gold and not afraid of encountering Tommy-knockers take note: As of this writing, the Crescent Gold Mine is for sale.

Joe Bush

Before leaving this area, let's consider Joe Bush. One haunt that is legendary here is the Sumpter Valley gold dredge that was used from 1912 to 1954 to extract rock and dirt from the river. According to legend, the ghostly Joe Bush has decided to stay with the gold dredge and is haunting it. Joe also served as a convenient scapegoat. It wasn't me—Joe did it! Whatever went wrong was blamed on him. How does one reprimand a ghost?

There is some debate as to whether Joe was a real person or someone created to frighten new employees. Mining was dangerous, no matter what job a man might have. The gold dredge that operated 24/7 was one of the more dangerous jobs. By sharing tales of Joe's grotesquely mangled body and ultimate death, mine supervisors hoped to keep safety uppermost in their crews' minds.

Get near the dredge if you dare, but you should know that Joe considers it his own and might not take kindly to anyone he thinks is encroaching on his property. Of course, he may just be a legend—or not.

Mt. Hood and Columbia River Gorge

Hood River Hotel

The Hood River Hotel is situated in some of Oregon's most picturesque spots. Built in 1888, in proximity to the train station, the
hotel was called Mt. Hood Hotel. On November 17, 1910, a story in
the *Hood River Glacier*, the hotel offered a special Sunday dinner
complete with musical entertainment for 50 cents. Times change,
but Ola Bell, one of the hotel's earliest owners, isn't aware of that.

She died in 1942, but that hasn't stopped her from claiming room
319 as her own. Nor has it stopped her from roaming the hallways
of the hotel at all different hours. Those who've encountered her
say she nods and smiles warmly. They've no idea a ghost has just
greeted them—not unless they should turn back for a glimpse of the
old woman to find the hallway empty.

Chief Comcomly's Head

*E*very fan of ghost stories has no doubt read of the headless horseman who struck fear in the heart of Ichabod Crane in Washington Irving's 1819 classic *The Legend of Sleepy Hollow.* Nothing is more dreadful than a headless ghost that gets everyone's attention. It's hard to imagine just how a specter might have come to be separated from its head. And certainly no one wants to ask a ghost how they came to be headless in the first place. Nonetheless there is always a backstory.

In Chief Comcomly's case, there is also irony. The chief was dead many years before having the misfortune of losing his head. A grave-robbing doctor had no problem digging up Comcomly's grave and stealing the skeleton's head. But let us look at how this all came to be.

When Lewis and Clark arrived in 1805 in what is present-day Oregon, Chief Comcomly was the leader of the Chinook. A shrewd negotiator, the chief saw an advantage for the tribe and wasted little time in befriending the explorers. He did this against the wishes of some of his people who were mistrustful of the newcomers.

In his 1836 book, *Astoria*, Washington Irving—yes, the same creator of the headless horseman—praised the long-dead Chief Comcomly's diplomacy. Indeed, the chief's diplomatic skills were remarkable and had helped to keep peaceful relations between the Chinook and the Europeans.

In 1830, an epidemic struck the Chinook, claiming the life of Chief Comcomly. According to custom, the chief was buried in a canoe in the family's burial grounds, but the chief would rest peacefully only five years before he was subjected to the worse disrespect imaginable. In 1835, as he was preparing to leave Oregon, Dr. Meredith Gairdner stopped at Chief Comcomly's burial site and stole his skull. The package containing the chief's skull was then sent to

England for study. Gairdner would not live long enough to reap any benefit for his outlandish theft. He died five months after robbing the chief's grave site.

Later Chief Comcomly's skull would be studied and displayed at the Royal Naval Hospital Haslar Museum in Gosport, Hampshire.

American Indians consider stealing from the dead one of the most unconscionable crimes anyone could commit, and this may be why Chief Comcomly was thought to be the shadowy figure that silently walked the area of his canoe memorial in search of his head.

One hundred and eighteen years later, Comcomly's skull, somewhat damaged during the Blitz in World War II, made its way back to Oregon in 1953. Here it was put on display at the Clatsop County Historical Society Museum. From there it was sent to the Smithsonian, and the ghostly Chief Comcomly remained headless.

The Chinook requested that the skull be returned to them for burial. In 1972, the skull was finally returned and buried with the chief's remains.

Western Oregon

A Ghost Walks at Mahonia Hall

*P*oliticians come and go; ghosts not so much, at least not at Mahonia Hall, which is the official residence of Oregon's governor. Although there is no ghost hunting permitted at Mahonia Hall, the place has long been rumored to be haunted, especially the first floor.

Built in 1924 by businessman, hops grower, and Salem mayor, Thomas Livesly, it was 60 years before the home became the residence of the Oregon governor. This was because after a 130 years of statehood, Oregon decided it was high time the state provided a home for its governor. A contest was held to name the home; the public, excited at the chance to name its state's official residence, submitted several suggestions. A 13-year-old boy won the contest with the name Mahonia Hall. Why Mahonia, you ask. *Mahonia aquifolium* is the Latin name for Oregon's state flower, Oregon grape.

One of the ghosts in residence is the home's original owner Livesly himself, who died in 1947; the home remained in the family until 1958. Those facts seem to have escaped Livesly who is said to haunt the master bedroom early in the morning and the first floor of the mansion late at night. Previous residents of the mansion warned governor Neil Goldschmidt that Livesly's ghost appeared at regular intervals in the master bedroom around 7:30 in the morning. Some said the ghostly Livesly appeared in a black robe, and others said it was grey. Most agreed Livesly seemed to be unhappy.

Goldschmidt laughed the stories off. As of yet, no governor has admitted to encountering ghostly activity at Mahonia Hall. Some things are best left unsaid—perhaps, especially in view of poll numbers.

Camp Adair

*C*amp Adair was larger than any city in Oregon, except Portland. Once known as Oregon's second-largest city, today is known as Oregon's largest ghost town.

With Hitler in power and the Nazis marching across Europe, the need for a US army training facility was obvious. After considering other sites, the military selected an Oregon location six miles north of Corvallis. Its terrain and climate were similar to that of Germany, where it was assumed fighting would take place. The need for the military's proposed training facility intensified with Japan's surprise attack on Pearl Harbor on December 7, 1941.

Within six months of the Pearl Harbor attack, the military began clearing the way for houses and farmland to be purchased from residents, many of which came from families that had lived in this region since the 1800s. With the country at war, there was no choice, and these families were forced to sell and relocate elsewhere.

Wells was a small community that happened to be in the pathway of the proposed camp. Slated for demolition, its railroads would be rerouted. The only buildings in the way of the camp's construction that weren't razed were churches. They were given to communities throughout the area. Some still exist today. Once the acreage was cleared, the US army quickly established and constructed a 57,000-acre facility, calling it Camp Adair in honor of Henry Rodney Adair, a member of a prominent Astoria family, and an officer in the 10th Cavalry, who was killed in the 1916 during the Mexican Border War.

Camp Adair, known as Swamp Adair to the enlisted men, was a boost to the local economy. From 1942 through 1944, more than a 100,000 soldiers trained for combat at Fort Adair. More than 40,000 people once lived and worked here, and some of them are still here. Unaware that the war is over, these ghosts of long-dead men go about their daily routines. The ghost of a German prisoner of war also walks these lonely grounds as the wind whispers through tree-tops. A wildlife sanctuary now, if you listen closely, you can also hear the POW's sorrowful cries. He never made it back to his homeland and remains here in this land of strangers forever.

The dead were also affected by relocation. According to the Camp Adair Sentry from September 10, 1942, 12 cemeteries (and more than 600 bodies) would be moved and combined into one cemetery to clear the way for the new facility. The story goes on to say that some of the headstones had burial dates that went as far back as 90 years.

The estimate was high. Only 414 graves were relocated from the Smith Cemetery in Lewisville Cemetery to a new Smith Cemetery, which is located across the street from the Fircrest Cemetery in Monmouth. A posted sign indicates that this area is relocated from the Camp Adair area in 1943.

As paranormal researchers know, relocating the dead like this may be expedient, but it is never a good idea.

A corner of Camp Adair was incorporated as the city of Adair Village in 1976. Although most of the old camp's buildings were destroyed or removed, a few of them remained. It was at the crumbling Camp Adair prisoner of war hospital that two ghostly prisoners of war were sometimes seen. Occasionally the whispered sounds of someone speaking German were reported at the old site as well.

Professor George Harding and the Ghosts at Western Oregon University

He who dares to teach must never cease to learn.
—John Cotton Dana

*E*stablished in 1856, Western Oregon University (WOU) is located in Monmouth, about 12 miles west of Salem. Billing itself as the safest university in Oregon, WOU can also be proud of its graduation rate of recipients of Pell Grants and of being the first-ever winner of the Higher Education Excellence in Diversity (HEED) Award in 2012. WOU's campus is charming, and it would seem that the university's ghostly inhabitants agree with me on this.

Perhaps they stay here at WOU because they have taken John Cotton Dana's words to heart. Learning doesn't stop—even in the afterlife. Our ghost quest begins at Todd Hall, which was originally a women's dorm and was named after dean of women, Jessica Todd, who came to work here early in the 1900s when it was the Oregon Normal School, a school that trained high school graduates to be teachers. Todd helped with fundraising that enabled the building of Todd Hall and the cottage in 1912.

She was a stern woman who had strict rules and woe to those who disobeyed any of them. Her punishments could be severe and extreme. She would not permit men into the dorm, and even today men have reported feeling unwelcome and ill at ease in Todd Hall.

"I didn't see her, but the feeling was intense all the same," said one student who claimed to be uncomfortable whenever he visited Todd Hall.

Others have seen her in the hallway, and the encounter includes an immense chill that wafts through the air as the scowling bespectacled Todd checks on her charges. Don't tell her that she retired from the university 90 years ago or that she's been dead since 1944.

She is a ghost on a mission. Ghost researchers tell us that we retain our same personality traits in the afterlife, so it's no wonder she isn't smiling.

Thomas and Carrie Gentle came to Oregon from Illinois to teach at the Oregon Normal School in 1911. Three years later, they moved in the Gentle House at 855 Monmouth Ave. N. Built circa 1880, the house would remain in the family until Catherine Gentle gave it to the university for events in 1981. Today it is an event center, a garden, and museum that can be rented for weddings and other special private events.

The house was a fitting gift because the Gentle family was long associated with WOU. And yes, the house is the residence of the ghostly Catherine Gentle, who likes wandering through it, turning lights on and off. Other than that bit of mischief, she is a sweet ghost.

Rice Auditorium was built in 1976, seven years after theater professor George Harding died. The 26,000-square-foot auditorium is used for theatrical performances and purposes. And it is where the ghostly professor is usually found. Harding was devoted to teaching theater and drama. He loved his job, his students, and WOU. Shortly after his death, strange noises began happening in the building where he taught.

When Rice Auditorium was completed, the ghostly Harding moved in. He is responsible for odd, unexpected noises, unexplained drafts, and changes in the lighting.

The Phantom Bugler of Forest Grove

Fare thee well,
Day has gone,
Night is on.

—From *Taps*

*P*resent-day Forest Grove in the Tualatin Valley was inhabited by the Atfalati, a tribe of the Kalapuya American Indians until settlers began coming to the region in 1840. Sometime later came the tale of the phantom bugler. He is said to inhabit the forest around Forest Grove, and he is pure evil. Anyone that happens to be in the forest around Forest Grove after dark should be careful if they hear the sound of a mournful bugle. That is the only warning the phantom bugler gives before he attacks.

Like so many other ghost tales, there are several variations to the legend of the phantom bugler. According to one story, he was an old man who lived alone in the forest long ago. Wherever he went, his bugle went with him. And that was fortunate the morning he was attacked by a mountain lion. The old man saved his life by battering the big cat to death with his bugle. He survived, but he didn't come away unscathed; his face was badly scarred and his mind shattered.

Soon he was hunting people in the forest much as the mountain lion had hunted him. When he came upon anyone, he killed them with his bugle, hiding their bodies so that they were never seen again. One winter night, a storm swept across the valley, and torrential rains sent everyone scurrying to the safety of their homes. But there would be no refuge for the murderous old man. This was the night karma caught up with him.

The fire had gone out in his stove long ago; he was too frail and sick to build another one. He lay there in his bed overcome by coughing and shivering as an icy wind whistled through the cabin's chinks.

He died there alone in his squalid cabin. Rather than being the end of a madman's reign of terror, this was the beginning of the tale of the phantom bugler.

Death had claimed him, but they say the melancholy sound of the old man's bugle can still be heard on clear moonlit nights. He's an evil ghost. And he uses his unearthly bugle to lure the curious to his ghostly trap. Once he is upon someone, the ghost beats his victim to death with that same bugle.

McMenamins Grand Lodge

*I*f you happen to be in the Forest Grove area for the antique shops and wineries, this quirky hotel is one of those places you really shouldn't miss. Originally built in 1922 as a Masonic lodge for the poor infirm and aging members of the Masons and their families, the Grand Lodge offers one-of-a-kind artsy and comfortable rooms. If you're wondering whether the place is haunted, remember that there is a ghost log for guests to record their encounters with the lodge's ghosts. The most famous of the bunch is called Anna by some and the Lavender Lady by others.

A painting that hangs in the Grand Lodge is said to be the likeness of the elderly lady who spent many years at the lodge. It wasn't long after her death that she began appearing in the hallways. Some say she even dances her way up and down the hallways. But just to be sure that she isn't missed, the fragrance of lavender hangs heavily in the areas where she is most often spotted.

Listen! Over in the nearby children's cottage, do you hear it? That's not the sound of wind whispering across the treetops. What you're hearing are ghostly children laughing and playing much as they did in life.

Vera at Knight Hall

Where words leave off, music begins.

—Heinrich Heine

She is quite famous locally. Everyone in Forest Grove knows who she is; she's Vera, the ghost who haunts the top floor of Knight Hall at the Pacific University. Beyond that, Vera stories vary, depending on who is telling the tale. According to one story Vera was a young music student who played the piano and sang when Knight Hall was the university's school of music; she died accidently in the building. Another tale has Vera dying elsewhere and returning to Knight Hall. It is also possible that Vera isn't even the ghost's real name. She may have been a resident here in the late 1940s when Knight Hall was still a women's dormitory. All that seems to be certain is that she's here and has been for a long time.

Still there is the matter of the ghostly music that occasionally echoes through Knight Hall. It's Vera, they say, playing the piano. Those who've heard her play say she does so well. And that's no easy feat, considering there is no piano in the building.

Vera is a multitalented ghost who sings as well as she plays. Her disembodied laughter is often heard in the old building, especially after one of her pranks like moving things around, turning lights off and on, and opening and closing doors.

Oregon Coast

Newport's Haunted Lighthouse

Situated at Yaquina, on the coast of Oregon, is an old, deserted lighthouse. It stands upon a promontory that juts out dividing the bay from the ocean, and is exposed to every wind that blows. Its weather-beaten walls are wrapped in mystery. Of an afternoon when the fog comes drifting in from the sea and completely envelopes the lighthouse, and then stops in its course as if its object had been attained, it is the loneliest place in the world.

—From "The Haunted Light at Newport
by the Sea" by Lischen Miller

In 1899, Elizabeth Maude "Lischen" Miller's story "The Haunted Light at Newport by the Sea" appeared in the August issue of *Pacific Monthly* magazine.

In her story, Miller, the sister-in-law of noted Oregon writer, Cincinnatus H. "Joaquin" Miller, told of something unworldly going on at the lighthouse on Yaquina Bay. In doing so, she has enchanted and perplexed ghost investigators ever since. Although the story was never said to be anything other than fiction, there were many that believed it was true.

Newport's Yaquina Bay Lighthouse was built in 1871 and served until 1874. Today it is Oregon's only existing wooden lighthouse and also the only lighthouse in the state with its living quarters attached. Some believe it to be the oldest building in Newport. Aside from Miller's story, there is Captain Evan MacClure and the tale of a ghostly construction worker who wanders the lighthouse stairs in search of his body that was somehow trapped between the walls.

Young Muriel Trevenard is the protagonist of Lischen's short story. And she is the ghost most people want to encounter, even though she sprang straight from the writer's imagination. In the story, Muriel and her friends go to explore the haunted lighthouse. Before they can encounter any ghosts, the fog starts rolling in and they decide to abandon their plans and leave. This is when Muriel notices she's left her handkerchief and goes back inside alone to retrieve it.

She is never seen again. For some inexplicable reason, Muriel disappears into the haunted lighthouse, leaving only her blood-stained handkerchief behind. Besides the handkerchief, there is the legend of blood stains on the floor that cannot be washed away. And oddly, hundreds of people claim to have encountered the ghost of Muriel since the publication of Miller's story.

My family and I have visited Newport many times over the years. While there, we invariably make a trek to the Yaquina Bay Lighthouse. We agree that there is something eerie in the old building. The ghostly inhabitant is a ghost who pops in and out of the lighthouse. While we've never seen an apparition here, we've felt its presence. And although we realize it isn't the fictional Muriel Trevenard, we have asked if the ghost is that of the unfortunate Muriel. As yet we've not received a response to our question.

Neither have we encountered the captain of the whaling ship *Monckton*, Evan MacClure, whose mutinous crew set him adrift in a dingy at Devil's Punchbowl in 1874. The ghostly redheaded captain is said to have roamed the coast of Oregon before settling in at the old lighthouse. Captain MacClure wanders the area around the lighthouse, greeting anyone he happens to meet. No one has a clue he is a ghost, and apparently, that is how he likes it.

Several years ago, there were news stories about a group of Canadian researchers that had successfully created a ghost, calling him Philip Aylesford. Perhaps with so many wanting to experience a ghostly encounter with the misfortunate Muriel Trevenard, another ghost has decided to step in and give the public what it wants.

> "It will be a dreadful blow to her father," remarked the landlady of the Abbey Hotel, "I don't want to be the one to break it to him." And she had her wish, for the sloop nor any of its crew ever again sailed into Yaquina

Bay. As time went by, the story was forgotten by all but those who joined in that weary search for the missing girl.

But to this day it is said the blood-stains are dark upon the floor in that upper chamber. And one there was who carried the little handkerchief next to his heart till the hour of his own tragic death.

Heceta Head Lighthouse Bed and Breakfast

*T*here are those who consider Heceta Head to be the most haunted place in the state of Oregon. It is certainly one of the most picturesque. Located at Devil's Elbow state beach halfway between Florence to the north and Yachats to the south, the lighthouse was built in 1894. Named for Portuguese explorer Don Bruno de Heceta who set out to explore the Pacific Northwest in 1775, the Heceta Head Lighthouse saw many lighthouse keepers come and go. When it was automated in 1963, the need for a keeper ended.

You may feel a chill or hear a disembodied voice while touring the lighthouse, but those working here will be quick to tell you there are no ghosts. If you're looking for ghosts, check the former lighthouse keeper's house, which is now a charming bed and breakfast. That's where the ghostly action is. A ghost by the name of Rue is said to haunt the bed and breakfast, and she's been at it for several years. Who is Rue and how do we know her name? Legend has it that a Ouija board spelled out the name of R-u-e one night when sitters asked for her name.

There are many stories and variations as to Rue's identity. She is said to be the young daughter of a lighthouse keeper who disappeared one stormy night. Another tale has Rue as the mother of a young girl who drowned near the lighthouse. There have been sightings of both a young girl and an elderly woman dressed in late 19th-century fashion that appears and disappears in different locations of the building.

There is also the party that takes place on the front lawn. It's a costume party, all participants are elegantly attired in a style of the late 1800s, and a table is spread with all manner of tasty cakes, cookies, and pies. A little black terrier runs about, yapping happily. Look closer! This is no costume party; those are all ghosts, including the little dog. Did they live here at one time? Are we witnessing a time warp, or is this a group of ghosts enjoying an afternoon at the lighthouse keeper's house?

Hitchhiking Ghost Lady of Siletz

*N*o one likes driving across the old bridge in Siletz late at night. If you're doing so, be aware that you just might encounter the hitchhiking ghost lady. Local lore sometimes refers to her as the Klamath Lady. The story is that she jumped to her death from this bridge and has been hanging out here ever since. That's one story anyway. The other has the woman's husband angrily pushing her from the bridge. The facts of just how she met her death have long since been lost. She's dead, but she's looking for a ride.

So let's suppose that you come on her one night and choose to drive on by. Bad decision; according to legend, those who pass by without acknowledging her will crash their cars in the next few hours. Just to be on the safe side, you might stop and offer her a ride. She'll silently slide into the backseat and travel with you for a short distance.

You look in the rearview mirror and ask, "How far are you going?"

The backseat is empty—; you're alone in your car. She's going further than you intended driving tonight. And as chill bumps rise up on the back of your neck, assure yourself that you're not the first person to take this ghostly hitchhiker for a ride—and you won't be the last.

Ghost Ship of Siletz Bay

*O*n fog-shrouded nights when the bay is calm, it appears but only for one brief moment—a ghostly galleon adrift in Siletz Bay at Lincoln City. By the time you've got your binoculars out, the ghost ship has disappeared.

With thousands of sailing vessels shipwrecked off its coast, the Oregon coastline has been referred to as the Graveyard of the Pacific. Which of those unfortunate ships haunts Siletz Bay? Is the ghost ship somehow connected to the three mysterious shipwrecks: the *Blanco*, the *Uncle Sam*, and the steam tug *Fearless*?

The brig, *Blanco,* was sailing from San Francisco to Coos Bay when it somehow got off course and wrecked off the coast in 1864. Or it may have been the 113-ton schooner *Uncle Sam* that wrecked off the coast in 1876.

The steam tug, *Fearless,* met its doom in 1889, and it's doubtful it would be mistaken for one of the other sailing vessels. Still, it is connected to these three mysterious shipwrecks that occurred 13 years apart. But where were the ships' crews? There were no bodies. When a ship wrecks, debris, flotsam, and bodies wash ashore. But there were no bodies to be found in the wreckage of the *Blanco*, *Uncle Sam*, or *Fearless.*

Any one of these doomed crew members could be at the helm of the ghost ship that sails Siletz Bay—a ghostly reminder of just how unforgiving the sea can be.

North Lincoln County Historical Museum

The late Dave Oester, Oregon ghost hunter, said that ghosts are everywhere. I think he was right in this. But here I will hasten to add that some places are more haunted than others.

Museums by their nature fall into this category. They are, after all, the repositories of historic items and the belongings of dead people. Who is to say if a ghost has decided to cling to a treasured object that once belonged to them? And who is to say that a ghost might simply be enjoying hanging out in the museum with familiar objects?

Disembodied voices and footsteps have been heard at the museum by those who work late at night. Sightings have been reported on the second floor of the museum as well.

Alonzo Tucker

Those who can make you believe absurdities, can
make you commit atrocities.

—Voltaire

*O*f the 21 lynchings that took place in Oregon, that of Alonzo
Tucker is the only lynching of a Black man in the state's history.
And it may well have resulted in an angry ghost who walks the area
seeking justice that eluded him in life.

On September 18, 1902, a cruel and terrible injustice befell
Tucker. Tucker was lynched from a bridge in Marshfield, which is
Coos Bay today. Gymnasium owner and boxer, Tucker was inno-
cent. He begged them to listen to him. His words fell on deaf ears.
A white woman had accused a Black man of raping her. Without
benefit of judge or jury, he was guilty because the mob proclaimed
him so.

"It wasn't me. I'm not the man you want," Tucker cried.

No one listened to him. Their collective mind was made up and
the angry mob pulled him from the jail. As he struggled against the
crazed men, one of them shouted, "He's trying to escape!"

Another pulled a gun and shot Tucker twice, once in the leg and
once in the chest; he died of his injuries as they dragged him to the
bridge. It didn't matter to these men with racist hatred coursing
through their veins.

A noose was slipped around Tucker's lifeless neck, and he was
lynched in broad daylight. So sure of their righteousness that not
one member of the mob hid behind a mask. And yet, when asked
later, no one remembered seeing a thing nor could anyone point out
those guilty of the murder of Alonzo Tucker.

Tucker's lynching is a wrong that can never be righted. This
doesn't mean that honor cannot, and should not, be paid to a man

who was cruelly murdered long ago on the word of one person without benefit of a trial. In 2020, the city of Coos Bay began telling Alonzo Tucker's story in the museum and with a plaque near the location of his death. There are plans to erect a statue in his honor as well.

Perhaps this is why the misty apparition of a man occasionally appears near the area where Tucker was lynched. Those who've seen him say he seems confused and angry. He may be seeking justice and the clearing of his name.

Manzanita's Ghost Pirate

O Gold! I still prefer thee unto paper.

—Lord Byron

*M*any centuries ago, a Spanish galleon came slowly into Smuggler's Cove and dropped anchor. It was a pirate ship and it would be here only briefly because there was work to be done. A small crew carefully lowered a chest into a rowboat. They then stepped into the boat and the sculler began rowing toward shore. Overhead, the full moon cast dancing lights across the water. No one spoke; the only sound was water lapping against the boat. Once ashore the men moved swiftly, struggling with the weight of the chest they carried. At the base of Neahkahnie Mountain they stopped, put their load down, and looked around. Picking up the chest once again, the men slowly made their way up the slopes.

They had found their spot. They stopped, put the chest down, and began the task of digging. When the hole was finally deep enough, they pushed the chest into it. But the task wasn't quite finished. Before any of them had time to think, one of the men pulled his dagger from its sheath and plunged it deep into the chest of another man. He explained to the others that this was the only way to protect the treasure. After all, who would disturb a grave? The dead man's body was pushed in on top of the chest and the hole was covered over.

Their chore completed, the pirates stopped to study the landscape, consigning the spot to memory. Satisfied that they would be able to find the location of the buried treasure chest on their return, they made their way back to the beach and their awaiting boat. As the wind picked up later in the night, the galleon's anchor was ordered aweigh and the ship sailed off into the night.

What the pirates hadn't realized was that several members of the local Clatsop tribe had watched their every movement that night—even the slaughter of one of their own. The tale of the buried treasure and the ghostly pirate that guards it would be passed down from one generation to the next in the Clatsop tribe. And as time passed and more people came to settle this region, even those outside the tribe came to know of the buried treasure.

The story varies according to who is telling it, but the legend remains. And thus, the question as to who would disturb a grave has been answered. Apparently, all bets are off when it comes to buried treasure. Countless people have come to Manzanita in the past hundred years, dreaming of untold wealth. In their endeavor they may encounter a ghostly, red-eyed skeletal pirate who stands guard over the beach and the hidden treasure said to be buried somewhere on the slopes of Neahkahnie Mountain. He is an angry ghost who was slain to protect the treasure of another, and he does this very well. Some say his unearthly shrieks are the reason the treasure has never been located.

Compelling as it may be, many believe there is no buried treasure, and the story is nothing but lore. This does nothing to stop the stream of 21st-century gold seekers who come each year with their equipment, their maps, and their dreams. One day someone may discover the buried treasure and walk away a wealthy person—if they can avoid the ghostly pirate that guards it.

Grumpy's Ghost

There is no love sincerer than the love of food.
—George Bernard Shaw

If you're in the market for breakfast grub or something sweet and sticky you should know about Grumpy's Café in Rockaway Beach. It's a little family-run café with an array of goodies. Just looking over the bakery offerings at Grumpy's will set a sweet tooth into high gear. I'll put those cinnamon rolls and nicely frosted donuts on my must-have list and tell you about the ghostly man who's made a home for himself at Grumpy's.

He's been there for a long while, even before the café itself. No one knows his backstory, and so they've given him the name Roger. It's a good name. And he's popular with patrons who come for the pancakes and for a glimpse of him. But ghosts don't appear simply because they're asked to do so. And, certainly, Roger has no intentions of making an appearance until he wants to.

Perhaps Roger is the ghost of Sterling Hays a newlywed who tried to show off to his bride by swimming way out beyond the breakers. Weak and unable to return to shore, Hays perished in the icy waters. His body was never recovered.

Whoever he may have been in life, Roger enjoys moving things, turning lights on and off, and turning water taps off and on. I don't know why it is, but ghosts seem to have a propensity for moving things around. Perhaps this is easier than making appearances or speaking.

Tioga Building at Coos Bay

*A*t nine stories, the Tioga Building in Coos Bay is the tallest building on the Oregon Coast. Listed on the *National Register of Historic Places*, the building was begun in 1925, but it wasn't until 1948 that it was complete. The Great Depression and World War II interrupted its completion. If you're looking for a place to rent, the Tioga Building offers studio and two-bedroom apartments. Who knows? You may even meet a ghost or two.

Recently upgraded, the Tioga is rumored to have secret passageways and several ghosts on the premises. And yes, they have been spotted throughout the building.

McAuley Hospital

*G*hosts are everywhere. But do they remain even after the building they've haunted is demolished? We're about to find out. The McAuley Hospital in downtown Coos Bay was built in 1925 as the Wesley Methodist Hospital. Four years later, the Sisters of Mercy took it over and changed the name to the McAuley Hospital.

After a remodel in 1982, the old hospital became the Ken Keyes College. The college was closed in early 1990, and after a succession of owners, the building remained empty for the next 20 years.

This is when the ghost stories started. Indeed, the forlorn old building did have the look of a creepy haunted hotspot. It wasn't long before sordid tales of ghostly mad surgeons who committed horrible atrocities on their patients and screaming ghosts began to infiltrate the building. The basement, it was said, was the residence of a ghost so evil no one dared to go down the stairs and see for themselves; no one, except ghost hunters that is.

Those who were fortunate enough to get into the building told of seeing and hearing ghosts throughout. A pitiful sobbing man walked in and out of empty rooms. A nurse with a white cap in thick soled white shoes silently trod the hallways going about her tasks. But most ghost investigators could only dream of going into the old hospital. All the while the building was vacant and for sale.

Then in 2018, the Oregon Health and Science University bought the building. That same year the old hospital was demolished to make way for student housing that will be built there. The question is, will the ghosts move on with the rubble that once was McAuley Hospital or will they stay in the same location unaware that things have changed? I'm betting they will stay put, but only time will tell.

Neskowin Ghost Forest

*I*n a book of ghost stories, this one is not what you think. The ghosts at Neskowin are primeval and have been carbon-dated to at least 2,000 years old. The remains of an ancient Sitka spruce forest stand on the beach like sentinels guarding against everything but time—the one thing that cannot be conquered.

These once majestic trees stood nearly 200 feet tall when an earthquake suddenly ripped the land apart swallowing the forest. The trees remained hidden here beneath centuries of sand and mud, only a legend—, until 1997–1998 when a series of violent storms pounded the coast, tearing away the sands that had hidden the trees.

Who walked among this ancient forest? I wish that had been my thought the first time I saw the Neskowin Ghost Forest—it wasn't. I didn't know this was the remains of a more than 2,000-year-old forest that is about 11 miles from Lincoln City. Coming back and walking among these ghosts is on my list of things to do—when the tide is out, of course.

Van Duzer Corridor

This stretch of Highway 18 near Lincoln City seems to be a potpourri of paranormal activity. Named for Henry B. Van Duzer, a member of the Oregon State Highway Commission and first chairman of the Oregon State Parks Commission, the scenic roadway is only 12 miles long, yet there are a number of locals that will not drive it—day or night.

There are just too many strange things taking place on the roadway. According to local lore, the strange assemblage witnessed on Van Duzer Corridor includes the elusive Bigfoot who has been known to stop traffic as he crosses on and off the highway.

Like Nevada's Area 51, it's said that a secret government installation is located somewhere within the Van Duzer Corridor. The first clue is the strange flying crafts that occasionally hover, lights flashing, over Van Duzer Corridor. Unafraid of UFO activity, ghosts appear and disappear along the highway as well.

A luminous man has been seen standing in the middle of the highway only to disappear as vehicles approach. No, he doesn't run to the side of the road. He simply disappears in a whirl of vapor. Ghostly hitchhikers are popular along roadways across the country. Where are they going and why do they need a ride? While we ponder that, I'll tell you that there are a couple of haunted hitchhikers in the Van Duzer Corridor.

A woman and a small child, standing forlorn and lost on the edge of the roadway, pull over and stop if you must. But I wouldn't advise it. They are ghosts with nowhere to go as you'll soon discover. The temperature in your car will drop the moment you stop and open the door for them. You won't get far before you realize your passengers are no longer in the car with you.

Now you know why many locals just won't drive the Van Duzer Corridor.

Bob Everest Fire Station

*A*lso known as the Oceanlake Station, the Bob Everest Fire Station is where the district's administrative offices are located. Here you'll find the offices of the fire chief, the deputy chief, the fire marshal, and a ghost. It's one of those stories that have been told for a while now. According to local lore, the ghost of a volunteer firefighter is still on duty at the station on the north side of Lincoln City. Some say he died of a heart attack in the fire station; others claim he died elsewhere and has returned to keep careful watch over the fire station that he loved.

But everyone needs a break during the workday or night, even ghosts. He's been spotted lying on the sofa in the break room and also on the firetruck. When he isn't seen, the ghostly volunteer's footsteps can be heard throughout the station as he makes his rounds.

Wildflower Grill

Ghost hunting gourmands take note: If you're in for a scrumptious breakfast or lunch, let me tell you about the Wildflower Grill in Lincoln City. This little eatery offers an array of dishes for breakfast and lunch.

I'm up for the seafood omelet myself—topped with the Cajun hollandaise. Ummm, that fresh crab and shrimp is out of this world. After a bite or two, I'll start looking around for the ghostly Matilda. Will she make an appearance? I hope so, especially now that I know she is the friendly sort. Chances are she won't show up. Her appearances are as rare as natural pearls, considering that only 1 in 10,000 oysters will yield a pearl. Still, we can hope for a glimpse of the elusive Matilda.

At one time Matilda was guilty of pinching the derrieres of people just for the fun of it. With time, she's mellowed and changed her ways. And now, she enjoys opening doors and moving things around. This might be a nuisance at times. It's still better than some of the meanies that haunt other places.

Matilda may not have been her name in life, but she seems to accept this moniker with good grace. She may not have even lived here; like us, she is drawn no doubt by the ambiance and the aroma of home cooking.

Snug Harbor Bar and Grill

So a ghost walks into a bar.

*I*f you're looking for Taft you should know that the small town was merged with Delake, Oceanlake, and the unincorporated communities of Cutler City and Nelscott in 1965 to become Lincoln City. And it's here in the Taft district of Lincoln City, that you'll find the oldest continuously operating bar on the Oregon Coast. It is 90 years old and still going strong.

Every town has its neighborhood bar and grill where locals like to gather for a good time. The Snug Harbor Bar and Grill or the Snug, as locals call it, is just such a place. Music, beer, cocktails, and food served up in a convivial atmosphere—what more could you ask—a ghost perhaps? Not to worry, one long-told story is that the Snug is home to a rollicking fun-loving crowd of ghostly lumberjacks and seamen. And once the bar is closed for the night, and the living leave the premises, the ghosts come out to party and have a good time without being bothered by the constraints of the living. Serving up the libations for the crowd from the hereafter is the Snug's famous barefoot bartender.

When the mood strikes him, the ghostly bartender does occasionally make an appearance early in the evening, but don't start calling out your drink orders to him. He prefers the company of his ghostly customers. Other bartenders may refuse to serve spirits to spirits, but he certainly doesn't. Ghosts can handle their boos.

Depoe Bay Winery

*T*he city of Depoe Bay is especially popular with whale watchers who come from all over the world to see the whales. The little city is home to what they proclaim to be the world's smallest navigable harbor that covers approximately six acres and measures about 50 feet by 100 feet. And, of course, there is the spouting horn, an ocean geyser, the only one within a city limits on the Oregon Coast and one of a few found outside of Hawaii. If you stop to take a photo, prepare to get soaked as the water rushes in and rises up in a watery wet spray.

Across the street from the spouting horn are shops and restaurants—and ghosts. The Spouting Horn restaurant is closed at this writing. It was a popular eatery with locals and tourists. In residence was the ghost of the old sea captain whose apparition often appeared to people throughout the restaurant. There are claims that the ghostly sea captain was actually filmed in action.

Described as having flowing, white hair and an angry countenance, he took pleasure posing at the windows late at night. And if that wasn't enough to frighten people, he hid utensils and tools necessary to prepare meals.

Wine tasters take note: the Depoe Bay Winery is just up the block. Some say there is a ghostly resident attached to the winery, which is affiliated with the Nehalem Bay Winery. The ghost at the Depoe Bay Winery has been here for a long time; a ghostly young man who seems to enjoy his surroundings very much, he seldom makes appearances but those who are sensitive to such things say he is always smiling. And why wouldn't he be here at the winery?

Uppertown Firefighters Museum

*D*o you want to see some old firefighting equipment, like a 1921 Stutz pumper or an 1876 LaFrance Hook and Ladder Truck? The Uppertown Firefighters Museum is the place; this old building in Astoria started life as the North Pacific Brewery established by John Kopp in 1884. Five years later, it was Astoria's largest and most successful business. That same year the brewery was destroyed by fire. The brewery was rebuilt and would continue operating until Oregon enacted the nation's first state Prohibition act on January 1, 1916, and the brewery's doors were closed.

Three years later, on October 28, 1919, Congress enacted the Volstead Act (Prohibition) making alcoholic beverages, their manufacture, and distribution illegal. There would be no coming back for the North Pacific Brewery.

In 1928, the city of Astoria converted the brewery to serve as Uppertown Station #2; it would remain in operation for the next 32 years. Legend has it that sometime during that time, a fireman accidently fell to his death in the building.

It wasn't long before the other firemen began suffering from strange experiences that wreaked havoc with their sleep. The unfortunate fireman's ghost was making appearances at their bedsides on certain nights. When he didn't appear to them, his disembodied voice would be heard. No matter how well you liked your coworker, this can be unnerving.

In 1990, a new and modern fire station was built and Upper Station #2 was converted to a museum. Today the museum boasts a large collection of antique firefighting equipment including a couple of trucks from the 19th and early 20th centuries.

Oh, and if you're wondering what became of the ghostly fireman, word is, he remains on duty to this day—and night. His footsteps are often heard on the third floor and occasionally disembodied laughter echoes through the old fire station.

Handsome Paul

*T*he Liberty Theater, in the Astor building, is nearly a century old and is listed on the *National Register of Historic Places*. Opening night was in 1925, three years after the devastating fire that swept through Astoria on December 8, 1922, destroying 30 city blocks, and the Liberty has been a favorite of theatergoers ever since. You can bet that big box of buttered popcorn that some of these theater fans are from the afterlife.

Our first theatergoer from the hereafter is called Handsome Paul. And the elegant Paul knows how to haunt a place in style. His choice of attire is always a glowing white tuxedo and a panama hat. The flashy Paul has been here and haunting the historic Liberty Theater in Astoria for a long time. Looking around at this beautiful theater it is certainly easy to see why he stays on.

Perhaps you will be one of the lucky ones that catches a glimpse of the ghostly Paul. If not, you will know he is in attendance and up to his old tricks if you should hear knocks and shrieks and notice theater lights turning themselves on and off or items that move about on their own.

Those who've seen him say he is indeed handsome and seems to be a happy ghost. Perhaps he was a movie buff who spent happy hours here rubbing shoulders with many of the rich and famous of bygone eras. Whatever his reason for being here, Paul is not the only ghost residing at the theater.

There is also the specter of an elderly woman who glides up and down the aisles in the early morning hours. Like Paul, she knocks on walls and moves items around. She is trying to let everyone know she's ready for her close-up. Will someone please let Mr. DeMille know?

Peggy and the Haunted Chair

*O*ur daughter-in-law comes from a long line of Oregonians. This is one reason our family spends a winter vacation week on the Oregon Coast every year. We rent a house in different small towns, stock up on a good supply of groceries, and proceed to enjoy the week with Peggy leading us on sightseeing trips around her state, while enjoying each other's company and the beautiful coast.

Recently we stayed at a lovely house in Seal Rock right on the beach. On the first night, Peggy commandeered a lone recliner/rocking chair that sat facing the window. Placing her phone, her tablet, her diet coke, and other Peggy paraphernalia down, much as one might place a flag of ownership on an unexplored land, she told us this was her chair for the duration.

The next night, after a wonderful home-cooked meal, we sat in the living room laughing and talking. Suddenly Peggy cried, "Look! Look at this chair!"

The chair was slowly turning—first to the right and then to the left.

I grabbed my phone ready to capture the moment on video. The chair stopped moving.

"Are you doing that, Peggy?" I demanded.

Her expression told me she was not. I put the phone down, and we continued our conversation. "Look!" Peggy said. "It's doing it again."

And it was. Once again, I picked up the phone. And once again the chair stopped turning.

This happened off and on for the next week. We would all watch in amazement as the chair moved. But the moment one of us attempted to capture it on video, the movement stopped.

Although we tried to get an explanation through electronic voice phenomena (EVP), there was nothing—; no other paranormal activity took place in the house that week. When told about the incident later, a friend suggested that the ghost may share similar energy with Peggy and that is why it moved the chair. Either that or the ghost was simply having a little fun at our expense.

Ghosts at the Argonauta Inn Beach House

*N*ever turn your back on the ocean; Oregonians know this all too well. They are also aware of sneaker waves, so is anyone who has ever visited the Oregon Coast. Sneaker waves are unpredictable—and deadly. These large powerful waves can rush in unexpectedly and pull a swimmer, beachgoer, or even a small craft out to sea in the blink of an eye. So, although there is no denying that the Oregon Coast is breathtakingly beautiful, it can also be dangerous; it is always wise to heed the warnings that are posted at the locations where sneaker waves are known to occur.

Most of the drownings that have happened at Cannon Beach are probably the result of a sneaker wave. Early in the 1970s, a family was enjoying the day at the popular Haystack Rock near Cannon Beach. Suddenly, without warning, a sneaker wave swept both parents far out from shore. Rescuers recovered their bodies several hours later. In spring 1988, a tourist from Washington was standing on a cliff at Hug Point State Park when a sneaker wave pulled him out to sea. His body was spotted in the water, but by the time rescuers got to it, it had disappeared. The cautionary tale of a careless man is the basis of our next ghost story.

The ghost of this man has played a starring role in the nightmares of coastal Oregonians for more than six decades. You will have no trouble recognizing him. He is the lonely gray ghost who walks Cannon Beach in the wee hours as he makes his trek to the Argonauta Inn Beach House. The extent of his travels is from the beach to the beach house. Once inside the beach house, he is known to move things around and lock and unlock doors and windows. Some, who are sensitive to such things, have felt a strong sense of foreboding when the ghostly man is active.

Did such a person exist? I wanted to know. And I don't call myself a researcher for nothing. I searched through countless old files and newspapers and could find nothing and certainly no drowning victim who perished under these circumstances. Even so, he may have been a real person, or he may have been someone parents created to keep their children ever vigilant and aware of the ocean's dangers.

As the story goes, he came alone to the Cannon Beach area one day in 1952 and checked into the Argonauta Inn Beach House. The next morning, a terrible storm was battering the coast. Everyone scurried to safety far from the churning ocean—except for him. He was curious and wanted a closer look at the enormous waves that were crashing ashore. He was warned. But against the advice of those wiser to the ways of the ocean, he pulled his boots on, grabbed his jacket and his camera, and walked out the door. Hoping to get some great shots of the waves as they struck the shoreline, he was oblivious to the danger and got too close.

He was never seen again. When the storm eased up a search was conducted. But there was nothing of him. It was assumed that he'd been swept far out to sea. Not long afterward his ghost returned to Argonauta Inn Beach House.

Most people agree that there is a ghost at Cannon Beach, although there are different theories as to who the ghost might be. One story holds that the ghost is a former owner of the beach house who roams this area, checking to see that his place is being well cared for. Meanwhile the ghostly man continues to haunt Cannon Beach and the nightmares of coastal Oregonians.

Bandage Man of Cannon Beach

*A*nother ghost that takes up space in the nightmares of coastal Oregonians is the infamous Bandage Man. Bandage Man menacingly wanders the roadways of Cannon Beach, the star of a story that's been told for decades. Since the ghastly tale began shortly after the death of a logger who was killed in a horrific sawmill accident in 1950, it is believed that the unfortunate logger may be the ghostly Bandage Man.

It's been estimated that Bandage Man is larger than the legendary Sasquatch that roams Oregon's wooded areas. Is he? He has been described as being large and taller than average height, covered in bandages from head to toe like a mummy. Better hold your nose if you should encounter him; they say he smells of rotting flesh. He is not your new BFF. There is nothing friendly about him. Locals know that Bandage Man is cantankerous. He will climb through windows and walk through open doors whenever he feels like it. He has also been known to smash the windows of slow-moving cars and to crawl into the back of pickup trucks and convertibles.

There is a road that the locals call Bandage Man Road. Off the beaten path and not widely traveled, the name alone is enough to keep me from driving it. But this is where Bandage Man has been spotted countless times. As is the case with most ghosts, Bandage Man is nocturnal and prefers to do his roaming on moonless nights. So if you should go looking for him in the afternoon, you probably won't find him.

But wait! Why would you go looking for such a nasty phantom as that of Bandage Man in the first place? Surely he is camera shy. And his stench is enough to make anyone keep their distance and it is probably something no one wants in their vehicle. Hang all the air fresheners you want; they probably won't help.

Tillamook Rock Lighthouse

*G*iven all the shipwrecks and tragic deaths that occurred on their doorsteps, you just know there must be a ghost skulking about at a lighthouse. In fact, ghost researchers and investigators think that lighthouses tend to be haunted. Having encountered a full body apparition at a lighthouse, I'll agree with that. There is no telling what I might encounter if I could only visit the lighthouse at Tillamook Rock. Tillamook Rock is a part of the Oregon Coast National Wildlife Refuge Complex managed by the US Fish and Wildlife Service. Unfortunately, no one, and this includes writers of ghost stories, is permitted to visit.

Long before a lighthouse was thought of, American Indians regarded Tillamook Rock as a cursed and dangerous place to visit. Locals call the lighthouse "Terrible Tilly" for the perilous conditions surrounding the lighthouse. Surprisingly, given all the danger, only one person lost their life in the building of the lighthouse at Tillamook Head.

John R. Trewavas, a 38-year-old master mason from Portland, holds this dubious distinction. On September 18, 1879, a storm was brewing when his surf boat arrived on the eastern face of Tillamook Rock. Trewavas was no stranger to the hazards of the ocean and carefully placed one foot on the rock. It was slippery. And somehow Trewavas lost his footing and was swept out to sea. His body was never recovered.

Some say that Trewavas has returned to Tillamook Rock. It's possible he is one of the ghosts who walk this forlorn old lighthouse. There are other ghosts here as well. Among them may be the ill-fated crew of the *Lupatia*, a British barque ship that crashed near Tillamook Rock 18 days before the lighthouse was lit.

The *Lupatia* had long since lost its captain, out of Antwerp and was fresh from Hyogo, Japan. Taking Captain Irvine's place at the helm was the ship's mate, B. H. Raven. On January 3, 1881, a dense fog obscured the moon and stars. Gale-force southwesterly winds churned the sea. When Raven realized that the *Lupatia* was sailing too close to shore, he called to his crew for help in righting the ship.

As Raven and the crew struggled to right the ship, the men at the lighthouse saw the ship's red light and heard their distressed voices and cries. They sprang into action, hanging lanterns in the lighthouse windows and hastily building a bonfire. They hoped that they could thwart disaster and guide the ship away from Tillamook Rock. Their efforts were futile.

By daybreak, the storm had passed. That's when the bodies of all 16 of the *Lupatia*'s crew were discovered strewn along the shore. There was only one survivor of the tragedy—, a young German shepherd, who had served as the crew's mascot.

It has been more than a century since that night in 1881, yet the ghostly *Lupatia* can still be seen thrashing against storm-tossed waves on certain nights. The harrowing cries of men, whose fates were sealed long ago, are carried along on the wind. And then, as quickly as the phantom ship appears, it vanishes, and all is silent once more.

Known as the loneliest lighthouse, Tillamook Lighthouse was so desolate and dangerous that wives and families of the keepers were not allowed to live on the rock. Because of this rule, four or five keepers usually lived on the rock at a time. The desolation could still be unbearable for some. Tillamook's first lighthouse keeper, Albert Roeder, lasted only four months before resigning in despair. Tillamook was just too unbearably lonely for him.

Years later, on a cold and dreary day, waves lashed against the lighthouse and a keeper went stark raving insane, grabbed a carving knife, and threatened to slaughter the other keepers. He was eventually subdued and sent to an insane asylum where he spent the rest of his life.

During its 76-year operation, from 1881 to 1957, lighthouse keepers and staff have told of seeing a ghostly ship out in the sea and apparitions in the lighthouse. Strange ghostly noises were sometimes heard as well. Two ghosts are said to be former lighthouse keepers who liked their jobs so much, they stayed on. Still others are believed to be some of the crew members of shipwrecks that occurred at Tillamook Rock.

But there is yet another more modern story that some might see as strange at Tillamook. In 1980, a group purchased the abandoned lighthouse and converted it to Eternity at Sea Columbarium. At this writing, some are spending eternity in the columbarium at Tillamook. But don't make your reservations just yet; honorary lighthouse keepers (cremains) are no longer being accepted.

If NASA can carry the ashes of Gene Roddenberry and his ilk to burial in outer space, I see no reason why a lighthouse can't be a columbarium.

More than 800 years ago, Geoffrey Chaucer wrote the poem "Troilus and Criseyde," expressing the sentiment that all things must come to an end. In Dr. William Colby Cooper's small 1904 book titled, *Immortality: The Principle Philosophic Arguments for and Against It,* the idea is expressed more succinctly with the phrase, "Whatever has a beginning has an end."

And so it is with this expedition into Oregon's ghosts. It ends here at Ecola State Park in Cannon Beach with its unsurpassed view of Tillamook Rock a mile away.

I thank you, dear reader, for joining me in this adventure. It's been a pleasure exploring the marvelous state of Oregon's fascinating ghosts and their stories; I sincerely hope that you have enjoyed the journey.

Bibliography

Books

Baker, John H., *Camp Adair: The Story of a World War II Cantonment*

Bowmer, Angus L., *As I Remember, Adam: An Autobiography of a Festival*

Burt, Christopher, and Stroud, Mark, *Extreme Weather*

Byrd, Joann Green, *Calamity: The Heppner Flood of 1903*

Chipman, Art, *Tunnel 13: The Story of the DeAutremont Brothers and the West's Last Great Train Hold-up*

Cobb, Todd, *Ghosts of Portland, Oregon*

Cooper, William Colby, *Immortality: The Principle Philosophic Arguments for and Against It*

Dawson, Charles, *Pioneer Tales of the Oregon Trail and Jefferson County*

Dearborn, Mary V., *Queen of Bohemia: The Life of Louise Bryant*

Eufrasio, Al, and Davis, Jefferson, *Weird Oregon*

Friedman, Ralph, *In Search of Western Oregon*

Gelb, Barbara, *So Short a Time: A Biography of John Reed and Louise Bryant*

Gibbs, James A., *Shipwrecks of the Pacific Coast*

Gill, Sharon A., and Oester, Dave R., *Twilight Visitors: Ghost Tales, Volume One*

Goodman, Kent, *Haunts of Western Oregon*

Goeres-Gardner, Diane L., *Necktie Parties: Legal Executions in Oregon, 1851–1905*

Gulick, Bill, *Manhunt: The Pursuit of Harry Tracy*

Hauck, Dennis William, *Haunted Places. The National Directory: Ghostly Abodes, Sacred Sites, UFO Landings and Supernatural Locations*

Helm, Mike, *Oregon's Ghosts & Monsters*

Holman, Frederick V., *Dr. John McLoughlin: The Father of Oregon*

Irving, Washington, *Astoria*

Jenkins, Arlene L., *Hauntings of Oregon*

Kitmacher, Ira Wesley, *Haunted Graveyard of the Pacific*

Laughead, W. B., *The Marvelous Exploits of Paul Bunyan*

MacDonald, Margaret, *Read Ghost Stories from the Pacific Northwest*

McCracken, Theresa, and Blodgett, Robert B., *Holy Rollers: Murder and Madness in Oregon's Love Cult*

Mills, Randall V., *Sternwheelers Up Columbia*

Morton, Marilyn, *Haunted Independence Oregon*

Myers, Arthur, *A Ghosthunter's Guide to Haunted Landmarks, Parks, Churches and Other Public Places*

Neal, Tom, and Scofield, Twilo, *The Well-Traveled Casket-Oregon Folklore*

Parkman, Francis, *The Oregon Trail*

Phillips, Jim, and Gartner, Rosemary, *Murdering Holiness: The Trials of Franz Creffield and George Mitchell*

Piggott, Charles Henry, *Pearls at Random Strung: Or Life's Tragedy from Wedding to Tomb: Including the Scientific Causes of All Diseases, Poverty, Premature Death and Longevity*

Ratty, Brian D., *Tillamook Rock Lighthouse: History and Tales of Terrible Tilly*

Reed, John, *Ten Days That Shook the World*

Riccio, Dolores, and Bingham, Joan, *Haunted Houses USA*

Shirley, Gayle C., *Four Legged Legends of Oregon*

Skinner, Charles Montgomery, *Myths and Legends of Our Own Land*

Skovlin, Jon M., and Donna McDaniel Skovlin Hank Vaughan, *1849–1893: A Hell-Raising Horse Trader of the Bunchgrass Territory*

Smitten, Susan, *Ghost Stories of Oregon*

Solomon, Grant, *The Scole Experiment: Scientific Evidence of Life After Death*

Stanford, Phil, *Portland Confidential: Sex, Crime and Corruption in the Rose City*

Stanford, Phil, *The Peyton-Allan Files*

Streckert, Joe, *Storied and Scandalous Portland, Oregon: A History of Gambling, Vice, Wits and Wagers*

Stewart, Donna, *Ghosthunting Oregon*

Walling, A. G., *History of Southern Oregon: Comprising Jackson, Josephine, Douglas, Curry and Coos Counties Compiled from the Most Authentic Sources*

Webber, Bert, and Webber, Margie, *Terrible Tilly (Tillamook Rock Light House): An Oregon Documentary: The Biography of a Light House*

Weeks, Andy, *Haunted Oregon: Ghosts and Strange Phenomena of the Beaver State*

Wright, E. W., *Lewis and Dryden's Marine History of the Pacific Northwest*

Magazines

The Atavist Magazine, Ghosthunter Leah Sottile, No. 99

BendMagazine.com, September 12, 2020

Oregon Historical Quarterly, Wendi A. Lindquist, "Stealing from the Dead," 2014, Vol. 115, No. 3

Oregon Native Son, June 1900, Vol. 2, No. 1

Oregon Native Son, September 1900, Vol. 2, No. 4

Pacific Magazine, Spring 2009, Vol. 42, No. 4

Pacific Monthly, 1899, Vol. 11, No. 4

Western Folklore, Pamela Jones, "'There Was a Woman': La Llorona in Oregon," July 1988, Vol. 7, No. 3: 195–211

Western Outlaw-Lawman History Association Journal, Spring 1997, Vol. VI, No. 1

Newspapers

Albany Democrat, April 20, 1922

Albany Democrat-Herald, May 11, 1982

Baker City Herald, October 2, 2019

The Capital Journal, October 15, 1938; January 30, 1952; January 11, 1964

Coast Mail, December 31, 1885

Corvallis Gazette-Times, November 13, 1922; October 31, 2002

The Daily Astorian, March 18, 1879

The Dalles-Times Mountaineer, May 22, 1897

Eugene Register, December 27, 1929

The Fort Wayne News, May 4, 1900

Heppner Gazette Times, June 18, 1903; October 26, 2005

Hood River Glacier, November 17, 1910

Lebanon Express, August 30, 1968

Madison Herald, March 20, 1886

Medford Mail Tribune, June 13, 1917

The Morning Oregonian, June 17, 1903

The Morning Oregonian, February 23, 1932

Oregon Daily Emerald, October 28, 1997

Oregon Daily Journal, May 2, 1906

Oregon Daily Journal, June 27, 1920

Oregonian, July 20, 1912

Oregonian, February 26, 1909

Oregon Sentinel, May 19, 1880; February 13, 1886

The Oregon Sunday Journal, June 27, 1880

Statesman Journal, October 31, 1981

The World (Coos Bay Oregon), October 31, 1987

The World (Coos Bay Oregon), February 14, 1989

Other

Douglas County Historical Society, Don Good, "The Brumfield Murder Case"

Oregon Historical Quarterly, Bob DenOuden, "Without a Second's Warning: The Heppner Flood of 1903," Spring 2004, Vol. 105, No. 1

About the Author

Janice Oberding is a Nevada-based writer. She enjoys traveling and researching history, true crime, and the paranormal. She is one of only a few people who have spent an entire night at Alcatraz—aside from those who were incarcerated there. She worked as consultant and historian for the Alcatraz episode of Syfy's *Ghost Hunters* (with Jason Hawes and Grant Wilson).

She has also worked with the History Channel, LivingTV, and the Travel Channel and has appeared in episodes of *Dead Famous* for Twofour productions, Travel Channel's *Haunted Hotels, Ghost Adventures,* and Fox's *Scariest Places on Earth.*

Janice has previously published spooky books with Stackpole, Arcadia/History Press, Pelican Publishing, and Fonthill Publishing.

When she's not writing, she teaches an annual ghost hunting 101 class for Truckee Meadows Community College's Paranormal Series. She also speaks at local events and paranormal conferences. Although she has had inexplicable things occur during her research, Janice remains a skeptic. You can find her online at Facebook.com/JaniceOberding and Twitter @JaniceOberding.